With My Hand in His

*A Collection of Inspirational Poetry,
Prose, and Other Ponderings*

Virginia Phillips Kreft

WestBow
PRESS
A DIVISION OF THOMAS NELSON

WestBow Press books may be ordered through booksellers or by contacting:

WestBow Press
A Division of Thomas Nelson
1663 Liberty Drive
Bloomington, IN 47403
www.westbowpress.com
1-(866) 928-1240

ISBN: 978-1-4908-0033-2 (sc)
ISBN: 978-1-4908-0034-9 (e)

Library of Congress Control Number: 2013913642

Printed in the United States of America.

WestBow Press rev. date: 9/26/2013

Foreword

Have you ever dreamed about sitting on a front porch swing, with the sun setting and the prairie stretched out before you? And what if the grandest of storytellers sits with you, reminiscing of a time gone by and bringing the past into the reality of today? That's what reading *"Ginna"* Kreft's recent book <u>WITH MY HAND IN HIS</u>, is like.

With the fluidity of a lifelong writer, Ginna brings you into the world of her longtime friends and family as they traverse the joys and pains of this world. Nothing is out of bounds as she whispers these stories into your ear. To give you even greater access into her life—and ultimately yours—you are treated to actual letters and poems written during the events to give clarifying light to the heart that is searching for, and finds meaning in, all that is happening.

Why should you read the story of someone you don't know? Because too many stories today are about what is wrong and how depressing life can be. Death, war, family struggles and a lack of resources penetrate our relationships and mindset. We are starting to believe the news that there is no way out. You need to sit down on the swing with Ginna and hear the stories of <u>WITH MY HAND IN HIS</u>.

Yes, they tell of death, struggles and a lack of things in this material world…but they don't stop there. Hope is given. Truth is brought back. Faith is paramount! She reminded me, and will remind you, that God is always faithful, your family is your strong support beam and a faithful friend sticks closer than any other.

I commend not only this book to you but a person. As you allow these words to speak, you won't see printed letters on a page. You will hear the voice of a wise friend sitting next to you on a porch swing as the sun sets.

—Pastor Joseph R. Fehlen, Author of RIDE ON: A Motorcycle Journey to Awaken the Soul and Rediscover its Maker.

Dedications and Acknowledgments

To Bill, my lifetime partner, my husband of nearly 59 years; father of my daughters, and my closest friend…How I wish he could see this finished project…Somehow I have this uncanny sense that perhaps in some way he can…

I still have moments of difficulty in realizing he is no longer here. I think I will always be aware of a special presence that more than fifty-eight years of loving each other has left with me.

His favorite chair is oh so empty,
And yet for a moment I see him there,
His voice no longer breaks the silence,
But his words of love still fill the air:

"Can I get you a cup of coffee?
Would you like me to get the car?
Leave that now, we'll do it tomorrow,
Please be careful, don't walk too far."

Yes, tears still flow, but tears can heal,
So I go on with joy in my heart,
More than fifty-eight years of caring and sharing,
Such sweet memories can never depart.

I decided to attempt putting this book together shortly before Bill entered the hospital for a relatively simple, outpatient surgical procedure. Following the procedure, things went awry and he never did return home to me. After thirty-six days in the Intensive Care Unit, Bill went home to be with the Lord. That was six months ago as I write this. I won't try to share here the necessary grieving process that my family and I are still working our way through —with God's help. Many of you have been there. Of course, my book was put on hold for a while. However, I knew I had to continue for several reasons, not the least being in honor of Bill...The initial decision to finally take the plunge, to *sign on the bottom line so to speak,* was the last major decision he and I were able to make together. I pray his faith in me will be justified. I'm so thankful for the patience he had with me for so many years—he has been a significant help in teaching me the benefits of Philippians 4:6: *"Be anxious for nothing..."* So, I will be anxious for nothing but to join him someday soon, when God also calls me home.

~~~~~~~

To my youngest sister Peg, who for years has kept asking, "When are you going to put a book together?" Three months after Bill's passing, before I could muster the desire to get back to this book project, it became obvious that Peg would soon reach the end of her brave 18 month journey with (inoperable/incurable) pancreatic cancer. With *her* hand in His, Peg went to be with the Lord less than four months after Bill. I am so grateful for Peg's inspiration...The courageous way she faced the seemingly imminent end to this life; and the shining example she left for us who still face that final journey. For *whatever reason,* God has already given me 13 years more on this earth than she had; and I'm keenly aware that I have procrastinated too long in compiling this book. In honor of Peg, I will try to be a better steward of the days I have left. When my time draws near, should I have to linger awhile—knowing as Peg knew...I pray that I can walk my final course displaying the same peace, faith and unwavering trust in God's sovereignty that she exhibited.

When does a sister become a friend?
Who but God can create such a blend?
Where does she become the best of you?
What is this bond that defines so few?
How do you go on when God calls her home?
With the same grace and strength she's so steadfastly shown.
Why will she really ne'er from you depart?
She'll always be with you—she lives on in your heart.

~~~~~

To the family most near and dear to my heart: My daughter Billie Jo and Grandson Alexander; my daughter Chrystina and Son-in-law Jeff. More than anyone else, this book is for you—your legacy in a way.

I would not have made it without you, this past year. Thank you—most of all for your love, it gives me strength; and for your unselfish, sometimes sacrificial support in so many areas of my life. You are *each* in your own individual way so very precious to me, and, of course, the "pride of my life." God blessed me abundantly when He made me your Mother. Dad was always so proud of you, and if he could see the way you *look out* for me in his place, he would be even more proud!

~~~~~~~

To Berniece and Ron, the most caring and supportive sister and "brother" anyone could ask for—thank you! Your contribution toward this book and my welfare will not go unnoticed by God.

~~~~~~~

To my very special niece Kendra and her husband Darrell. You have a special place in my heart, and always will. Thank you for your loving support.

~~~~~~~

To Helen, my dear friend and cohort in Christ, thank you for your support; for your help with proofing and your constructive critique. I will always be grateful God brought us together so many years ago. You have been a benefit to my life as well as this book. You are a treasured gift from God. *"Like God, you correct my mistakes. Like God, you do so gently—thank you for being so much like Him." (Borrowed from Max Lucado in LIVE LOVED).*

~~~~~~~

To each of my family and friends whose ardent interest and encouragement along the way have been a source of inspiration, especially when I got bogged down with the project—you know who you are!

Table of Contents

Foreword   v

Part One—A Word in Season—Presented in Prose, Poetry, and
Ponderings   xv

Preface   xv

Introduction—Part One   xxi
    Which Is Your Favorite?   xxv

Chapter One—Spring: A Time of New Beginnings   1
    Believe…   3
    Then Came the Rains   5
    The Certainty of Change   7
    The End Before The Beginning   9
    I Will Go On   10
    Goals and Methods…?   11

Easter   13
    What's In Your Alabaster Jar?   15
    More Than a Cliché   18
    Glory in the Cross   21
    For Me Alone   22
    A Resurrection Progressive   23
    When the Angels Were Silent   26

Chapter Two—Summer: A Time to Grow   29
    The Parable of the Pansy   31
    A Summer Treat—Taste and See   35
    Rooted and Built up   37
    Let The Sunshine In   39
    Hear the Daisies of the Field   42
    Beauty from the Storm   43
    Joy Comes in the Morning   45
    Take the Plunge!   46

Come To the Waters   49
This Is the Refreshing   50
Annual Church Picnic   52
Life-giving Aroma Therapy   56
On the Jericho Road   58
Higher Ground   60

Chapter Three—Autumn: A Time of Reflection and Transition   61
Autumn Introspection   63
Bring to the Storehouse   65
Romping   67
Stop, Drop, and Roll   68

Thanksgiving   71
Now I Lay Me Down to Sleep…   73
Assorted Shades of Grace   75
Thanks for the Memories   79
Heartfelt Thanks   81
Grace Comes Before Thanks-giving   81
To Thanksgivings Past   82

Chapter Four—Winter: Time for Rest and Reparation   83
Suddenly it's Winter!   85
Stand Still—Behold!   87
Be Still and Know   88

Christmas   91
The Incarnation   93
Optional But Essential…   95
Tell the Children   98
A Simple Advent Devotion   99
The Joy of Belief   101
Daystar   105
I Wish You Joy…   107

Happy New Year   111
My New Year Prayer for You   113
I Pray You Enough   114
A New Year—An Open book   115

Waste Not—Want Not   117
Would-a; Should-a; Could-a...   120
A Work in Progress   123
Today Is the Day...   125
Alone in His Presence   127

Valentine's Day—An Affair of the Heart   129
Magnified Through Love   131
Unfathomed—Unending Love   133
Do I Love Jesus?   135
A Friend Loves at All Times   136
Attitude Creates Reality   138

A Good Word for Any Season   143
Always Begin With Praise   145
The God of Abraham, Isaac and Jacob   146
Who Can Explain It?   147
One Night in May   149
My Daughter—My Friend   150
A Prayer for a June Bride   151
Two Roses   152
May Becomes December   154
My Husband   155
A Sacred Commentary   156
I Think I'll Get Radical   158
Final Moving Day   160

Epilogue   163

Part Two—Hope Lives On   165
Preface   167
Hope Lives On   169

An update...   185

Preface

I'm walking hand in hand with Jesus,
I'm trusting Him to lead the way,
I know that if I ever cling to Him
He'll never let me go astray...
Yes, I am walking and talking,
Walking all the way with Him.
—Unknown

This book is about a journey, mostly my own journey; but each of us must walk a similar path...And on the way, we share or cross paths with many who influence our walk to some extent. It is good to occasionally recall and thank God for such influences. To understand the meaning in the title of this book, it will help somewhat to have known and returned the deep love of someone special in your life (parent, first love, husband or wife...To have experienced the feeling of love, joy, security...of hope, promise, commitment and more...Simply in the way you can always sense them "grasping your hand tightly in theirs" as you walk the various paths of life. I have enjoyed the privilege of experiencing this daily in my walk with Christ... You've heard it said, in reality, <u>Christianity is not a *Religion*, it is a *Relationship*</u>...

Perhaps you have never had such an experience...then I invite you to let this book point you in the right direction...Jesus will fill that void—to full and overflowing.

This is not a novel and not something I recently decided to write—it is instead an anthology of things I've written over the years, primarily to and for myself, relating to my walk with God. Thoughts...about things I've observed, things I've heard, things I've learned along the way—from God, through His Word—His Spirit—His heart—His

Church. It has been a wonderful journey in both the good times and the not so good. Actually, I've probably recognized the Lord's presence more *up close and personal* "in the worst of times." Those times all the more strongly accentuate His grace, His power, His strength and His peace…And yes, His joy inexpressible. At 79 years old, I am *statistically* living on borrowed time; my journey will soon be over (and that will be glory)! So, if I'm going to do this book—I must get on with it.

As I look back on my journey, I can heartily say with the Psalmist, "You will show me the way of life…I follow close behind you; your strong right hand holds me securely." (Psalm 16:11; 63:8 NLT) I see oh so clearly now, that I probably would not have made it this far, had I not walked this path *with my hand in His*…You know it is said, "Hindsight is always 20/20!" Therefore, I see now why things sometimes went wrong—I had probably let go of His hand. And, of course, there were other times I carelessly loosened my grip…Ignoring the warnings, I stumbled on rocks in the path and suffered the consequences. (Psalm 91:11-12)

It's much like a young child walking along the wintry street *lightly* holding her Daddy's hand—she begins to slip on a patch of ice—in that same instant, before she can fall, her father clasps her hand even more tightly, and with a gentle upward tug of his strong arm she is safely upright once more. Grasping *his* hand a little tighter now—she skips along gleefully, keeping in step with her Father. *"When I said, 'My foot is slipping' Your love O Lord, supported me."* (Psalm 94:18) Every time I think about taking a wrong turn in life, I feel that same familiar tug, and I can't go on, *unless* I *choose* to let go of His hand. If I hold on firmly, He guides me and makes my path safe. *"Mark out a straight path for your feet; then stick to the path and stay safe. Don't get sidetracked; keep your feet from following evil."* (Proverbs 4:26 NLT)

In order to walk hand in hand, *we have the responsibility to make a choice*—we must *choose* to place our hand in His. He is always there "reaching down" His hand for us; we need only to "reach up" and grab that nail-scarred hand and hold on.

Jesus reminds us in Matthew 7:13-14: *"Enter through the narrow gate. For wide is the gate and broad is the road that leads to destruction, and many enter through it. But small is the gate and narrow the road that leads to life eternal and only a few find it."* He waits at the entrance to that gate—with hand outstretched, hoping we will grasp His hand and enter.

Although I have known the Lord since childhood, I did not make a serious, comprehensive commitment to Christ until adulthood. I am so thankful for that day when I removed the blinders from my eyes and clutched tenaciously to His hand, determined always to follow His leading. When the way seems impassable, I can know as Isaiah did: *"The path of the righteous is level, oh Upright One, You make the path of the righteous smooth."* (Isaiah 26:7)

God has always led me in "paths of righteousness" in Him. As I have walked this pilgrim pathway, I've encountered obstacles I've had to climb over, under, and around; but mostly, I had to *go straight through*—many heartaches, sorrows, *dangers, toils and snares*—always *with my hand in His.* By His grace I've walked in the joy and peace He has promised: *"And the peace of God, that transcends all understanding, will guard your hearts and minds in Christ Jesus; You will keep in perfect peace him who is steadfast, because he trusts in you."* (Philippians 4:7; Isaiah 26:3) That peace is found in accepting the simple reality that *I don't need to understand—I just need to hold His hand.* I find in so doing—He will often give me some measure of understanding also.

There is one essential thing I have learned from my experience, based on obedience to God's Word and the wisdom gained from those years of experience: When we commit ourselves to the Lord without reservation of any kind, He guides our steps closely. *"Trust in the Lord with all your heart and lean not on your own understanding; in all your ways acknowledge Him and He will make your paths straight."* (Proverbs 3:5) The things that happen to us never happen merely by human design or coincidence—but providentially. No matter what we face at any juncture in this road of life we can declare with Paul: *"We are knocked down, but we get up again and keep going...."* (2 Corinthians 4:9 NLT) We may feel as though we have the weight of the world on our shoulders at times, but Jesus wants to help carry that burden. If our hearts are fully yielded to Him, He will guide every footstep.

In this book, I'll share in the form of prose and poetry the many thoughts I've pondered and recorded over the years—the where-what-and why of this walk—this life in Christ. With few exceptions, if any, each reflection is based on scripture and the still small voice of the Holy Spirit. He has always been right there, helping and guiding me as I sought answers to so many things…I have certainly *not discovered all the answers*, but I know personally Who has *all* the answers, and if I follow Him, He will always guide me in the best way to go.

> *"The Lord directs the steps of the godly.*
> *He delights in every detail of their lives.*
> *Though they stumble they will never fall*
> *For the Lord holds them by the hand."*
> —Psalm 37: 23-24 NLT

It has not been easy deciding which writings to include. Most are just simple tidbits designed to prompt you to see Jesus in all the small, every-day things of life; prompting you to examine each thought further—and perhaps to discover a new truth for yourself. I hope to encourage you to *seek for answers* in much the same way I have sought—and still do. I have tried to share an example of some of the roads we all must travel in life at one time or another.…Highways and byways…primitive paths, roads well-travelled, teeming freeways, convenient bypasses, and the uncharted trails through the jungles and forests. There are so many lessons to be learned along the way—all paths to victory in Him. "Thanks be to God, who always leads us in triumphal procession in Christ." (2 Corinthians 2:14) It is my intention to remind you of some of the essential but *uncomplicated* ways we can *walk in triumph*—according to God's Word.

The paths I have trod have not been so different from the paths we all must traverse in this world…Not unusual or extraordinary nor especially noteworthy. However, my journey has been and will continue to be…inscrutably contented, peaceful and exciting. All because of my constant travelling companion and guide. Since I often need written direction, I keep my instruction book near…close at hand and heart—God's Word…In reference to which he says: *"When you walk they will guide you; when you sleep, they will watch over you; when you wake, they will speak to (advise) you."* (Proverbs 6:22) He often reminds me, "The Lord is my Shepherd; I shall not want. He makes me to lie down in green pastures; He leads me beside the still waters. He restores my soul; He leads me in the paths of righteousness for His name sake…" (Psalm 23) Why don't you finish it my friend? This is your dwelling place also!

The following scripture found in Philippians 3:10 in the Amplified Version of the Bible, has been my heart's desire for many years—it is often in the throes of that deep desire that I have written much of what you will read here…

"For my determined purpose is that I may know Him—that I may *progressively* become more *deeply and intimately* acquainted with Him, perceiving and recognizing and understanding the wonders of His person, *more strongly and more clearly*…and that I may so share His sufferings as to be continually transformed in spirit into His likeness…" (Philippians 3:10 Amp)

A. W. Tozer said: "He (Jesus Christ) is a person and can be known in increasing degrees of intimacy as we prepare our hearts for the wonder of it." Uh-Huh! Therein is the crux of it—we must *prepare* our hearts.

After all these years I still must confess, just as Paul so ably and humbly admits: "I don't mean to say that I have already achieved these things or have already reached perfection! But I keep working toward that day when I shall finally be all that Christ Jesus saved me for and wants me to be. No dear brothers and sisters, I am still not all I should be, but I am focusing all my energies on this one thing: Forgetting the past and looking forward to what is ahead, I strain to reach the end of the race and receive the prize for which God, through Christ Jesus, is calling us up to heaven." (Philippians 3: 12-14 NLT)

It is my prayer that this book will bring you small moments of pleasure, helpful insights, and a deeper longing for a genuinely intimate relationship with Christ.

**God wants us to have more—
More LOVE...More INTIMACY...More
CONNECTION...More of HIM!**

Introduction—Part One

"To everything there is a season. . ."

A season for every activity under heaven...God has made everything beautiful for its own time.
—Ecclesiastes 3:1, 10

Season in the Bible refers to *any* passage of time, as well as to the agricultural cycles The ancients had no idea of the how or why of it. They knew nothing of the earth turning on its axis or revolving around the sun, creating a continual cycle of change. Yet they knew beyond a shadow of a doubt that the seasons would always come—always go, and that they could do nothing to slow them down or hurry them up, let alone stop the process—it is a promise of God. (See Genesis 1:14) As sure as God is, and He IS—spring will always come—followed again by summer, autumn and winter....

...And so it is with life—natural and spiritual—it not just an inert sequence of sameness; life is a journey of ever-changing seasons. However in our spiritual life, though we will experience all seasons, one may not always follow the other in precise order. Some seasons are anticipated and enjoyed, some are planned for, dreamed about...But some seasons come unexpectedly, with painful abruptness, some are dry—wearisome—even boring. God tells us He has made *everything* beautiful-*for its own time*...So what do we do until it is turned into His time of *beauty? That is when it is* all the more necessary to be looking to God, trusting Him to take us through each of the seasons—to not just survive, but thrive...He will bring us through productively—according to His sovereign will. How important it is to keep our faith built up (see Colossians 2:7), so we'll always have the strength to trust God through these difficulties of life. Nevertheless, one thing we *can* always predict with assurance—spring will always follow winter, even in the spiritual realm. Praise God for the promise of spring! God said, "As long as the earth remains, there will be springtime and harvest, cold

and heat, winter and summer, day and night." (Genesis 8:22 NLT). . .
So it is—both natural and spiritual. Just as in creation, the seasons God
takes us through spiritually are for specific purposes…to make us more
fruitful so, "We will be like trees planted by the riverbank bearing fruit
each season without fail." (Psalm 1:3 NLT)

In Spring, He plants in us the seed of His Word, and nurtures us in the
grace and forgiveness of His love.

In Summer, He prunes us in mercy and waters us in the living waters
of His Holy Spirit…to multiply our fruit.

In Autumn, In the midst of harvest, He encourages reflection on the
season past and preparation for the coming of winter. . .

In Winter, A time of rest, that may however, include…bitter cold, dark
barrenness; but—GRACE GROWS EVEN IN WINTER!

Perhaps you will find yourself portrayed, past, present or future, in
one or more of the seasons suggested in the following pages. You may,
of course, see your specific situation fitting a different season than I
have—but undoubtedly you *will* find you are in here somewhere—or
have been at some point. Wherever you find yourself—God is there
with you—if you keep your hand in His.

In relating God's Word to our life circumstances, you will notice I often
repeat some of the scriptures—some of the same analogies. This is in
part because the entries have been written over various periods of time.
Also, I have found that in dealing with us, the Holy Spirit is repetitive;
and the more often we grasp a truth from the Word—and prove that
truth in our lives, the sooner it becomes engrained in us—deep down
in our being, until it is as much a part of us as breathing, or our human
DNA—our spiritual genes you might say…In this way we begin to
more closely resemble Jesus Christ—Which is His loving will and desire
for us. I pray that is your desire.

~~~~~~~

"A word spoken in due season,
how good it is."
—Proverbs 15:23 KJV

"Pay attention my child, to what I say. Listen carefully.

Don't lose sight of my words.

Let them penetrate deep within your heart,

for they bring life and radiant health to anyone
who discovers their meaning." Proverbs 4:22

~~~~~~~

Which Is Your Favorite?

Winter is NOT my favorite season...as soon as Christmas is over, I'm ready for spring. The very sound of the word *(winter)* sends a chill up my spine. By the time February Second comes, I am not thrilled if the infamous Mr. Groundhog does not see his shadow! Nevertheless, I often think how blessed I am to live where we do enjoy all four seasons; I know that here in Northern Wisconsin the changing four seasons are a sure thing. I've learned to adjust to each one, to most certainly prepare. I enjoy the weather traditionally associated with each—though winter is a stretch...I can't imagine Christmas season without snow...

How grand it is to watch the change of seasons God so magnificently created. Think about it...with designated regularity, He splashes red and orange over green, and soon layers white over brown. After a time, once again, as sure as all of His promises, He will replace the drab gray of winter with spurts of green and yellow, like tiny fountains of new life—followed by the vast array of summer's brilliant colors. How faithfully He shows off the full spectrum of His handiwork...All with astounding detail that fills me with awe and hope year after year.

Of course, some may oft times wonder if we might do just as well without winter (especially we who are not winter sports enthusiasts). Nevertheless, each of the four seasons offers us its own special gift—if we take the time to notice and ruminate...And just as each of earth's seasons embraces its own sights, smells, feelings, expectations and benefits, and even disappointments—so it is with the seasons of life...

With winter comes the blessed holiday season. Thanksgiving and the glorious Christmas Celebrations! Followed by the lofty plans and dreams of a brand new year.

With that joyous but hectic, celebratory season behind us, it's a good time to do as nature does—rest. Take advantage of the shorter, slower, less demanding pace of winter…On a frigid snowy evening, sit long by a warm fire with a good book and relaxing music, preferably with someone you love…Look out and absorb the beauty of the snow-laden branches—like royalty draped in ermine. Note the soft, white blankets comforting the cold, barren ground. Take a walk and hear the quiet echo of the crunch of your footsteps as you stroll amid the falling snowflakes—Study your footprints—make a snow-angel.

Soon it's February, and we can thrill to a kiss from our favorite Valentine. Enjoy the assorted exchange of loving sentiments between family and friends…and don't forget to remind one another that "nothing can separate us from the love of God." (Romans 8:38-39)

Not any too soon, the howling winds of March are upon us, and we begin to anticipate spring…If we listen closely, we hear the breezes wafting a message of hope and promise—and *we can be sure* spring is just around the corner. What a difference perspective makes; and so it is in the seasons of life.

But, what if you've lost your perspective? Perhaps you're feeling a wintry-like barrenness in your soul in mid-July…Some days you can't help wonder where God is, why doesn't spring come? Take heart dear one, He is there, He knows, He cares. Believe His promise—such times will come—they are part of the seasons of life…They also pass and renewal takes place—as He promised. Just as with the earth, the bleakness of winter will pass, you will sense a new awareness of the warmth of the Son, of His love and presence…You will find refreshment, hope, and new fruitfulness.

God's promises have no expiration date.

~~~~~~~

<u>Spring</u>

A Time of New Beginnings…

To Till, To Cultivate

To Plant Seeds

To Feed, To Water,

To Pull Weeds

~~~~~~~

Believe...

"Ah, that is the reason the bird can sing; on his darkest days he believes in spring."[1]

THE FIRST DAY OF SPRING IS HERE! By the calendar that is, yet I see no sign...No tender shoots of green grass; no crocus resolutely pushing their heads through the cold, harsh ground. I hear no chirping of robins; the tree branches still hang gray and barren. All around the ground looks desolate, still held in the tenacious grip of dingy, ice-hardened snow.

Here and there in my little garden, a small spot has begrudgingly yielded to the penetrating warmth of today's sunshine, revealing the limp discards of last year's harvest. I'm trying to wrench from my memory a recollection of the bounty that flowed there last—the beauty and grandeur that once splashed in vibrant array across the flower beds...And in the garden—clusters of tender green beans, bright red tomatoes. Of course, I realize...*that* summer season is past, never to be reclaimed. I must let it go and wait instead for the promise of new joys...the promise of spring! I see no real sign, but I *will* believe God's promise—spring will come! As long as the earth remains, spring will follow winter. And thus we cry, "Lord, send the promise!"

For months now, the ground lay cold and dark in restful reparation—waiting to burst forth once more with new life and beauty. But first...there must be some cultivating to prepare the soil for the planting...Followed by faithful watering, feeding, and the tender care of a loving gardener.

And so it is with our soul—thus we cry, "Lord, I long to see spring—it's past time, Lord, and I see no signs! Help me, Lord, to have faith in your

---

1   unknown

promise." *"Now faith is being sure of what we hope for and certain of what we do not see. "The only thing that counts is faith expressing itself through love."* (Hebrews 11:1; Galatians 5:6)

"Faith is the bird that sings when the dawn is still dark."[2]

Soon I will feel the intense warmth of the risen *Son*, reaching deep into the drab recesses of my soul…penetrating, thawing, and reviving.

Yes, Lord, I will bask in the sunlight of Your love, while You restore, refresh, reseed. But first comes preparation of the soil. Yes, Lord, I will yield—in expectation of new life, beauty, and productiveness—all at the hand of the Father, my Master Gardener. (see John 15: 1-8)

"When the time is right, up springs life.
No manipulation, no control; perfect freedom, perfect liberty."
—Richard Foster

---

2   Rabindranath Tagore

Then Came the Rains

I will send showers—showers of blessing, which will come just when they are needed." —Ezekiel 34:26 NLT

Thank you, Lord, for the spring rains that come to help wash away all the drab and dreariness of winter's end, preparing for new life and new growth—Just the way You send the gentle, cleansing rain of Your Spirit into my life just as you said—at just the right time   Your time!

For instance, Lord—there was one special day, you remember—I know You were there too! I'll never forget that little freckle-faced girl, about six years old, standing inside the entrance door of the department store with her Mom, waiting for the pouring rain to stop. The kind of rain that is in such a hurry to touch earth it doesn't have time to flow down the spout, but gushes right over the top of rain gutters...I had my umbrella, but it was coming down so hard I decided to wait. We all waited—some patiently, while others seemed irritated that nature had disturbed their harried day. After a minute or so, some went running like antelope to their cars, as if hoping to run between the drops without getting wet; it seems they preferred being soaked to the skin to taking an involuntary respite. How sad that we've become so caught up in the worries and the busy-ness of the day, that we don't realize when God, through His creation, obliges us to take a brief reprieve—to see the wonder of getting lost for a moment in the sound of the heavens, washing away the dirt and dust of the world.

As I stood there watching and listening—memories of my running, splashing, carefree childhood came pouring in as a pleasant diversion from the ordinary concerns of the day. I even felt myself relax, calmed by the steady rhythmic sound of much-needed rain. The deluge became like a cleansing stream running down the slope of the huge parking lot. It seemed to be washing away all sorts of debris left behind by unconcerned litterers—empty paper cups, half-eaten sandwiches, candy wrappers, along with other miscellaneous remains. I found myself wondering what stories each bit of litter might tell about those in too big a hurry to stop by a trash container. The stream of that afternoon rain was sweeping it away—much, I thought, like Christ does for us (if we plead like the Psalmist), *"Cleanse me with hyssop and I will be clean, wash me and I will be whiter than snow."* (Psalm 51:7)

Suddenly my reverie was disrupted. . .

"Mom," the sweet little voice broke in, "let's run through the rain." 'No, honey,' Mom said, 'not quite yet, we'll get soaked if we run through it now.' "No we won't, Mom, no we won't," she said, tugging at her Mom's arm... "That's not what you said this morning, don't you remember? When you were talking to grandma about her cancer, you said, "If God can get us through this, He can get us through anything!"

Dead silence...Mom paused for a moment. What would she say—what could she say? She could confound her child's innocent faith, possibly causing permanent doubt or she could somehow enable it.

"Honey," Mom answered, "you are absolutely right—let's run through the rain. If God lets us get wet, well *maybe we just needed washing!"* And off they ran through the rain, stomping in the puddles, laughing all the way! Yes, they got soaked...

...And so did I, Lord; I decided to run also; carrying my umbrella on my arm, off I went. I got the message, Lord, through the faith of that child and her brave Mom—I needed washing!

Heavenly Father, remind me often to fold up my umbrella of complacency and take the time to sit under the rain of the Holy Spirit. May I become so sensitive to His ministry that I am always quick to yield—whether the rain is for some tending and watering, encouraging new fruit, or, if the downpour is intended to wash away the debris of life that I have carelessly allowed to accumulate...Oh, let the rains come, Lord!

The Certainty of Change

Changing weather—changing moods, changing seasons—changing times, just a few things over which we have no control! I have come to realize there is one sure and certain thing regarding our circumstances, whatever they may be right now—**at some point something will change.** Our lives will be rearranged time and again during our sojourn here on earth.

Some folks resist change of almost any kind. With a few exceptions, they want to hold on to the status quo—to live tomorrow just as they have today—and yesterday. They wonder why it can't be the way it's always been. It was good enough then, why not now?

They may realize that isn't realistic, yet you will never find them too far from their comfort zone. They don't seem to know that change is what fends off life's boredom. (*Is that perhaps why some folks are perpetually boring, they never move far from that old familiar, in a rut, comfort zone?*) Still others welcome the newness of change—always open to whatever God might have in store.

Some changes do bring unavoidable sadness, but in Christ, His comfort will minimize all grief, and it will pass—if we take God at His word. If, because of change, we find ourselves mourning over the loss of someone or something—then mourning is in order. Nevertheless, if we believe God, He will soon change that mourning into the oil of joy. (See Isaiah 61:3)

It is God's desire that we be *continually* changing—*for the better*—*in Him.* And how can we allow Him to fulfill His desire in us, unless we welcome, indeed *seek* such change? Lord, help us to embrace the words in 2 Corinthians 3: 18, and confirm those words in our hearts—declaring with expectancy, *"From glory to glory He's changing me!"*

In spite of perpetual change (which will continue until Jesus returns), we can be at peace. One thing in this world we know will never change is Jesus…Have a look at Hebrews 13:8: "Jesus Christ is the same yesterday and today and forever." The One who has never changed and never will—God Himself declared: "I the Lord do not change." (Malachi 3: 6)

A singer once said, referring to what makes beautiful music: "I can hold the same note for a long time; but eventually, that's just noise. The *change* is what we listen for. The note coming after that and the one after that and then the next and the next…That's what makes music!"

If we are to be a concerto to the Lord, we must allow Him to decide where to bring change…In our personal life AND in the Church—otherwise, we are *just so much noise.* So, friend, let the music flow—note to note, as we build to a harmonic crescendo! All under the direction of our Master Conductor! Embrace this changing melody called life; your part is essential, as is mine—together we can be a great symphony for God—His Masterpiece, under His direction—played for all the world to hear.

The Holy Spirit is the composer who can expand the song of the Lord through us, enabling us to join in heaven's song.

The End Before The Beginning

"I am God and there is none like me.
I make known the end from the beginning,
From ancient times what is still to come.
I say: my purpose will stand, and I will do all that I please."
Isaiah 46:10

The old at times must be virtually ended
Before the new can begin,
We often must know the sorrow of losing
To value what we might win.

"Remember not, things of old," says He,
"Trust for things ever new;
They will spring forth just as I have proclaimed,
When you seek me wholehearted and true."

And should the road seem too hard to follow,
God's ever faithful to you,
He'll provide the strength to follow Him onward;
He knows the best pathway through.

"This is the way, walk ye in it,"
We hear His voice from behind.
With that gentle voice and His strong hand leading,
The mountain's much easier to climb.

"God knows everything in one eternal now,
including the past, present, and future.
And God knows the future before it happens in time."
Norman L. Geisler

ONLY GOD can create the right beginning...*ONLY HE* writes the perfect end.

I Will Go On

When times are good, be happy; but when times are bad, consider:
God has made the one as well as the other.
—Ecclesiastes 7:14.

I will go on when storm clouds gather,
Jesus knows what lies ahead.
I will go on when sin o'erwhelms me,
He will forgive just as He said.

And when I'm filled with discontentment,
I'll not blame others, times or things;
I'll look inside—and let God search me,
Accept the answer the Spirit brings.

I will go on to know Him better—
His life, His death, more intimately;
Cleaving to Him, growing into His image,
Praying that others may see Christ in me.

I will go on to life abundant,
I in Him and He in me;
Joy and peace; a life o'ercoming,
For faith in Him spells victory!

"The Lord will make a way for you where no foot has gone before.
That which, like a sea, threatens to drown you, shall become
a highway for your escape." Charles H. Spurgeon

Goals and Methods...?

My God will perfect that which
concerns me. —Psalms 138:8 KJV

I said to the Lord:

I want to succeed, Lord; you know that I do,
A real turnabout, changed through and through.
I can't get there alone, Lord; I need Your assistance,
Put the pressure on, Lord, break down my resistance!

Destroy my self-seeking, topple resentments,
Suppress my fear, root out discontentment;
Carve away all pretense—burn up my vain pride,
Steady inconsistencies that flow with the tide.

And The Lord said to me:

I will cleanse you with My blood,
Overflow you with My love,
Direct you with My Word,
Grant blessings from above.

Invite you to My presence,
Where you can always be,
If you separate yourself
And cling first of all to me.

*Remember, "...my thoughts are not your thoughts, neither
are your ways my ways, declares the Lord."* (Isaiah 55:8)

You see, child, we have the same goals—
but you must trust Me to choose the methods.

In other words, Lord, like Joshua at Jericho...You will bring me through to victory in every battle if I let you plan and carry out the winning strategy.
Thank you, Lord, for—Assurance—guaranteed!

"We can gather our thoughts, but the Lord gives the right answer."
—Proverbs 16:1 NLT

~~~~~~~~

EASTER

Spells…

Eternal Life

~~~~~~~~

What's In Your Alabaster Jar?

While Jesus reclined at the table of a friend in Bethany, a woman called Mary came in. She brought with her an alabaster jar filled with a pound of expensive pure oil of nard (spikenard). With deep humility and abandonment, she broke the jar and poured it all out on Jesus; then loosening her long tresses, with great reverence she stooped down and wiped his feet.

(Compiled from the Gospels—various versions: See: Matthew 26:6-13; Mark 14:3-9; John 12:1-7)

...It was two days before Christ's crucifixion; Mary, a very devoted follower of Jesus, was already grieving. Some followers of Christ just hung around enjoying the ambience—curious of the aura surrounding this charismatic prophet. Others were sincere and wanted to be there when He became King...Surely it would be soon now, IF, He *was* the Messiah. He was, wasn't He? And He was here to deliver them from the horrendous bondage of the Romans! You see, many of them weren't really grasping what He was trying to tell them—they chose not to hear what He was saying—that He was about to die!

But Mary, having absorbed every word her Master ever spoke, had much insight. The others just didn't seem to "get it"; but somehow she sensed the reality of Jesus' impending death, even though she didn't fully understand. Even now Judas berated her over how much money they could have had in the coffers if she had given the oil to him to sell. The spikenard, probably imported from India, was very costly...forget the one hundred to two hundred dollars an ounce cost of perfumes like Chanel #5 or fragrances bearing the name of Armani, Lauren and today's other high fashion giants. Compared to this Nard stuff the Jerusalem business magnate was exporting, today's *top of the lines* aren't even close! It was so valuable, it was used for bartering purposes. Well-to-do parents gave it to daughters as a marriage dowry. It was probably Mary's life savings, surely her most valued possession. Still… she *broke* the jar and—LAVISHED ALL SHE OWNED—ON JESUS!

Jesus was deeply touched; He defended and praised her act of love…He even told the others it was her way of preparing Him for burial…then He declared she would always be remembered wherever the gospel is preached.

Reading the account again caused me to think…What's in my "alabaster jar"? Am I as selfless and devoted as Mary? Am I willing to give up something so precious to me, so supposedly costly—to honor God? What personal treasure am I holding back? Is there *anything* that keeps me from *surrendering all?* How about you, dear friend? What is the earthly treasure you're clinging to so tightly, holding back from Christ…Could it be as simple as our treasured time or money? Maybe it's that pair of "blinders" that allows us to overlook our lack of understanding, toler-ance…Some overdue apologies—perhaps some unforgiveness? What about *unceasing, free-flowing* praise and worship? Is that all "boxed up?" In these uncertain times—could it be you depend more on self and material things than on God? Do you fear "sacrificing to Christ" lest you lose too much "self"? He IS our "self"! *It is no longer I who lives, but Christ who lives in me."* (Galatians 2:20)

Much of what we "treasure" isn't at all valuable; we've just become attached to it and don't care to give it up. Undoubtedly, that thing we can't seem to relinquish to God is *more trash than treasure*—tucked away in the *facade* of our life—*our alabaster jar*…What secret part of us do we keep out of sight, never wanting it exposed to the light—those things we think are alright with God—yet we hesitate to practice in the presence of our church family? What is that *one little something* we keep holding onto? In essence we're declaring, "Lord, you're not going to get this! No-oo sir-ree! I want to invite you to once again review Colossians chapter 3 verses 5-14—you may want to make some spiritual wardrobe changes.

If we allowed God to strip away ALL façade, we might find ourselves naked before Him....Actually, that IS how He wants us—standing naked before Him; void of all our unattractive, ill-fitting cover-ups, so we can begin "putting on" these garments He designed for us. "Chosen of God for this new life of love, dress in the wardrobe God picked out for you..." (Verse 12 Msg.) But, even His garments can't really fit us well until we "put to death the sinful, earthly things lurking within us." (Verse 5)

I wonder, (salvation notwithstanding) do we fully understand the *true* purpose in God's heart for desiring that we have a *deep* relationship with Jesus Christ? That we become more and more like Him? Or are you still content with a very "basic" relationship? Are you just sincere enough with Him to "get to heaven"? Jesus desires to have a deeply intense, personal connection with us...Deep and Abiding—Familiar...*"In Him we live and move and have our being."* (Acts 17:28 NKJV)

Finally, Mary didn't just pour the oil out—she BROKE the container—to release every drop! When is the last time you were truly "broken" before God? Totally emptied of self...Longing to be "filled up" instead with the power of the Holy Spirit and love. *God loves a broken and contrite heart.* (Psalm 51:17)

Let's examine our hearts—take inventory. Break that secretly-treasured alabaster jar and pour it all out—at the feet of Jesus! He poured out His life's blood for us.

"Search me, O God, and know my heart;
Test me and know my thoughts.
Point out anything in me that offends you,
And lead me along the path of everlasting life."
—Psalm 139:23-24 NLT

More Than a Cliché

"April showers bring May flowers." Those were the first words that came to mind as I took pen in hand to record some thoughts on the wonders of spring, and the glory of the upcoming Easter Holiday Season. Quite catchy *I* thought—it *is* April after all, and those words were put to music years ago, and brought a guy named Al Jolson a lot of fame—and money! As I jotted down said words, my Alter Ego immediately responded with, *"Sounds a little trite, don't you think? You know—like a cliché?"*

Cliché! Do you mean like: a stitch in time saves nine...pretty is as pretty does...as old as the hills...? *"Uh...yes,"* she answered...And like: dead as a door nail...raining cats and dogs...every cloud has a silver lining...like that? *"Like that,"* Alter replied.

Trite? Well, even Shakespeare is credited with some well-known clichés—He wrote "to your heart's content...too much of a good thing... good riddance...love is blind...a sorry sight." Can you call Shakespeare *trite?* It all makes good sense to me. (Could that be why I seem to need an alter ego?)

So, I checked with Webster for the definition of <u>cliché:</u> *"A trite expression whose effectiveness has been worn out through overuse and excessive familiarity or a phrase that means something other than the literal meaning of the individual words."*

Now my mind really wanted to go off on a tangent...something doesn't quite jibe here. That definition of cliché could be attached to some things in the Bible—If Alter will let me be, I may be able to sort it out!

With all due respect to the Webster's, God's Word could never be "just a cliché". Although some statements in the Bible do fit, God's Word could never be considered *trite.* How about "a phrase that means something other than the literal meaning of the individual words"? Well, how about the parables of Jesus? And have you read the Old Testament Proverbs lately? In the Bible these words never *"lose their effectiveness"* and the more *"familiar"* they become, the more *effective* they will be in our lives. And—the Bible has been amazingly "effective" for many, many years, and will be for as long as this world remains.

So, just where does that leave us—concerning clichés and the Bible? In the Bible we find no *raining cats and dogs*—but I do recall quail…when the Israelites were miffed with God! You see, they were unhappy with what God had been providing for food, so, He *sort of—rained down quail!* (See Exodus 16:13)

Well finally, here we are, back to rain and showers—April showers.

"To everything there is a season." (Ecclesiastes 3:1) In Ezekiel 34:26 God says: "I will cause showers to come down in their season; there shall be showers of blessing." And He will do the same in your life. Of course, the "seasons" of our lives will not always coincide with the natural seasons, but God always knows what season we're in—He has allowed us to be there. That's why I like the above verse in the NLT; God says: "I will send showers, showers of blessing"…*"just when they are needed."*

And yes, *"every cloud WILL have a silver lining."* Also—*"it never rains but what it pours."* Lord, pour down the rain of Your Holy Spirit!

As we enter the Easter Season we need to ask ourselves—has the phrase "the cross of Christ" become little more than *a familiar cliché?* When you visualize the cross, does the image touch you at the deepest level of your soul and spirit? Has the *excessive familiarity* of the cross and Christ's horrible death allowed you to create a welcome detachment from the emotion it should cause within the very depths of your being? I believe we need to return regularly to the cross in our heart and mind (not just at Easter), and take time to grieve—over our part in His death; and receive a new awareness of the love that drove Him to that cross, where He died—for you—for me! Draw from that love *"to your heart's content"*. And remember, His *"love is (NOT) blind"*... Now **that's <u>more than a cliché!</u>**

In the old rugged cross stained with blood so divine
A wondrous beauty I see,
for 'twas on that old cross, Jesus suffered and died,
to pardon and sanctify me.

To the old rugged cross I will ever be true,
it's shame and reproach gladly bear;
Then He'll call me someday, to my home far away,
Where His glory forever I'll share.

So I'll cherish the old rugged cross, till my trophies at last I lay down,
I will cling to the old rugged cross, and
exchange it someday for a crown.[3]

---

3   *The Old Rugged Cross. 1913 by George Bennard*

Glory in the Cross

So oft in prayer I'd survey the cross
Of Jesus Christ with bitter remorse;
And think of the love that brought such pain,
Such sorrow and tears I couldn't contain.

My heart was o'erwhelmed with such despair
With grief, for my sin that held Him there.
As the nails bored His hands and tore His feet,
Saw His sword rent side…all the more I weep.

Piercing thorns became His crown,
As blood and tears came mingling down.
How can I repay the extravagant cost
You paid for me, Lord, on that cruel cross?

Then I heard Him one day
In voice gentle and sweet;
"The debt's paid in full,
The payment's complete.

Weep not my Child—in my cross rejoice,
Lest all be in vain—Lift up your voice!
Shout! Glory! Glory to the Father above!
Reflecting His glory, go forth, share His love.

*God forbid that I should glory, save in the cross of our
Lord Jesus Christ.* Galatians 6:14 NJV

Love so amazing, so divine—Demands my soul, my life, my all.

For Me Alone

If I were the only sinner in the world,
God still would have sent his Son;
If I alone were cut off from Him,
To earth Christ still would have come.

If only I were in need of a Savior,
Still my Lord would have bled and died;
Hanging there between heaven and earth
For my sins alone—crucified.

Yet my friend, for you, too, He died,
Rising Triumphant in glory and power;
The cost of our sin fully satisfied,
As He shed His life's blood in that hour.

For you and me—and the world dear friend,
He was sent from the Father above,
Dying alone His life He did spend—
Who can reject such redeeming love?

*"This is love; not that we loved God, but that He loved us
and sent His Son as an atoning sacrifice for our sins."*
—1 John 4:10

A Resurrection Progressive

I'm always pleased when the political elections are over for a while. Election time or not, it seems we are bombarded more each year, with *philosophically politicized* "labels". Some days I'm confused as to what is PC (politically correct) or PIC (politically incorrect)...Which one is it I'm supposed to be? No longer do we just simply have the traditional Democrat, Republican, Independent...Now there's the supercilious Liberals and steadfast Conservatives...they're divided even further—by extreme or moderate—far left or far right...radical or complacent—

And now we have the Tea Party...Occupy Wall Street...the 99%'ers, etc. And, then of course, there are the **Social Progressives**—A term I hear more and more these days...I don't believe I want to be one of those; however, I won't dwell on that right here and now—that enigma is not for here and now. I'm sure I fit into the above list somewhere—but not as a *Social* Progressive. However, like the apostle Paul, I am most certainly a **Resurrection Progressive**—And just what is a Resurrection Progressive? Paul explains in the Amplified Bible, Philippians 3:10-11...

"My determined purpose is *that I may <u>know</u> Him* (Christ)—that I may ***progressively*** <u>*become more deeply*</u> and *intimately acquainted with Him*—perceiving, recognizing and understanding the wonder of His person more strongly and more clearly; that I may in the same way *come to know <u>the power overflowing from His resurrection</u>;* and that I may so share in His sufferings as to be continually transformed into His likeness—even His death. In the hope that, if possible, I may attain to the spiritual and moral resurrection that lifts me out from the dead even while in the body."...That my friend, means *dying to self.* This is my desire—how about you?

From Father and Son Bible Scholars, the Blackabys:

"The cross and the resurrection began in the heart of God the Father, both were lived out in the life of Jesus the Son—but the full impact of both hits *our* lives. <u>Jesus died that we might live *for Him.*</u> The *power of the resurrection* is what the Father does in us when we die to self and choose to live in Christ. *You die; the Father resurrects*…He does not resurrect you to a *better* life primarily, but to a new life."[4]

> Resurrection is not just *heaven someday*, but *life today*—
> It is something believers experience in daily life,
> as well as something we'll experience for all eternity.

"He died for all, that those who live should no longer live for themselves but for Him who died for them and was raised again." (2 Corinthians 5:15) Paul said, *"I die daily…I have been crucified with Christ, and I no longer live, but Christ lives in me… I live by faith in the Son of God, who loved me and gave Himself for me."*
(1 Corinthians 15:31—Galatians 2:20)

<u>The Christian life is essentially a life of daily resurrection…</u>

The **power of the resurrection** is found in our ability to die. Jesus had to die for there to be a resurrection…and so must we. To be like Christ, we must first be—continually **(progressively)** transformed into His likeness—even His death—At some point we must come to the place that we can truly, with understanding, say, "I've been crucified with Christ."

Jesus said there *will* be a cross to bear, a denying of self…that anyone who wants to save his life, must lose it; but whoever loses his life for Jesus' sake will find it. (See Matthew 16:24-25) When you ask to *experience* the resurrection, you're asking God to take you beyond yourself. It will be costly, even painful at times—but the victory and the rewards are far beyond measure. Ephesians 3:14-21 is a good place for us to start claiming that! (See vv. 20-21) "Now to Him who is

---

4   Experiencing the Resurrection, by Henry and Melvin Blackaby; Multnomah Books. A division of Random House

able to do immeasurably more than we ask or think, according to His (resurrection) power that is at work within us."

"As we *progress* in the *resurrection* life, it not only leads us into an exciting walk with the Lord, it changes us deep inside. It begins to produce in us Christ-like character. We become a living example of the *power of the resurrection* to bring new life to that which was dead".[5]

> *Let me lose myself and find it Lord in Thee;*
> *May all self be slain, my friends see only Thee,*
> *Thou it cost me grief and pain, I will find my life again,*
> *If I lose myself and find it Lord in Thee.*[6]

Be a Resurrection Progressive!
Choose "life more abundant—with life eternal"!

---

5   Experiencing the Resurrection, by Henry and Melvin Blackaby; Multnomah Books. A division of Random House

6   Words by Ross H. Minkler; Singspiration Music/ Brentwood/Benson Music Publishers

When the Angels Were Silent

Come walk with me this Eastertide
To that night so long ago,
Young Mary with Joseph by her side,
The heavens all aglow

Hark! Hear Herald Angels sing!
Joy to the world they say,
All glory to the heavenly King
Who's born for you today.

Another night so long ago
In dark Gethsemane,
The world a Savior soon will know
He'll die—for you and me.

The Angels all are silent now…
God's Son dies all alone;
Redemption to the world endow,
Such love had ne'er been known.

"Tis finished!" The angels sing once more—
A song to set souls free!
He's risen! He lives forevermore,
He lives!—for you and me.

The angel songs come ringing by,
Resounding thru the years—
"Worthy the Lamb;" Who reigns on high,
God's gift to calm all fears

So at this great glad Eastertide,
We with the angels sing;
Our song shall evermore abide
Thru eternity 'twill ring!

"Day and night they never stop saying:
Holy, holy, holy is the Lord God Almighty,
Who was, and Is, and Is to come."
—Revelation 4:8

~~~~~~~

<u>SUMMER</u>

Time To Grow

To Be Pruned

To Enjoy The Bounty

~~~~~~~

The Parable of the Pansy

"Daisies don't tell," perhaps not—But Pansies do!

And what lessons they share...

Last summer we enjoyed the striking beauty of pansies in a large planter beside our patio. Lovely heart-shaped petals in velvety hues of deep purple, with centers that looked like little yellow faces...And bright golden ones, with small purple faces. They all survived so beautifully far into the fall, I wasn't in any hurry to pull them. But, of course, as autumn gave way to winter, they finally succumbed to the frosty nights. After the first snow fell, I finally pulled out the withered, frozen stems—we had seen the last of their royal beauty. They were annuals you see, meant to bloom only once.

We made our way through winter once again, and as March approached, we were gladly contemplating spring. In mid-March a spell of unusual summer-like temperatures of 70 and 80 degrees were a welcome surprise to all! The unusual warmth prompted an *added* surprise for us—one of astonishing beauty, pleasure- and some head scratching...We noticed what looked like pansies beginning to push their tiny heads up, reaching for the warm sun—creamy yellows and lavenders—pale, diminutive copies of their ancestors, struggling to grow—NOT in the planter—it sits there just as it did all winter, full of dry and barren soil. Instead, up through the *earth* they came—in the grassy strip between the planter and the rock bed; right at the very edge of the sidewalk—not an easy place to grow! Doesn't that put you in mind of the Parable of the Sower which Jesus told? (See Matthew 13:18-23)

In the weeks that followed, many more began to pop up, all neatly in a row as if a gardener had meticulously planted them that way. Despite a severe lack of water or nourishment (we didn't bother with them, we were sure they had no chance of surviving in such a place); they continued to thrive through several hard spring frosts. Growing just rapidly enough to keep their heads above the burgeoning sea of green grass—winsome, puffy little knolls of bright purple, yellow and white. These couldn't be the same variety I planted last summer, and yet they had to be. How could they change so? (Don't you think that's what Jesus means to do with us season by season…Transform us to look *and act* a little more like Him?)

Neighbors passing by often stopped to take it all in—with awe and wondering skepticism, perhaps questioning how and why…Why anyone would have planted flowers in the grass, at the edge of the walk—knowing the first time the grass is cut, they will be mowed down.

So, just what is their story? Jesus often used stories from nature to teach eternal truths; God still presents us with many such spiritual analogies—if we choose to recognize them. I find no less than 18 to 20 spiritual lessons in these pansies… For instance…Horticulturists describe pansies as: *a plant for all seasons.* Hmm, isn't there a scripture that tells us to be just that, "instant in season and out of season"? (2 Timothy 4:2) **Delicate:** ROGET renders that as tender, sensitive, considerate, tactful, graceful, subtle, diplomatic, discreet, and careful, among other interesting synonyms. (*Now,* how many scripture verses come to your mind?)

But, we've only just begun; this parable is full of comparisons of the life God desires for us as instructed in His Word. Yes, pansies are delicate—but also **hardy:** (robust, vigorous, strong)…They **complement any garden** arrangement; **do best on the fringes; grow to fullness without crowding out others**. (Could God show us any clearer, how to grow and bloom in Him—than He does through the pansies?)

And…Pansies have a very *delicate* **perfume-like fragrance**; As Paul says of us…"Everywhere we go people breathe in the exquisite fragrance. Because of Christ, we give off a sweet scent rising to God." (2 Corinthians 2:14 MSG)

Pansies **require a lot of water**; Jesus said, "If you are thirsty, come to me! If you believe in me, come and drink!" He was speaking of the Spirit. (John 7:37-39 NLT)…

…And **food**—*Your Words are what sustain me, they give me great joy and are my heart's delight, for I bear your name, O Lord God Almighty.* (Jeremiah 15:16 NLT)

Pansies **need the "full" light of the sun**, *Awake O sleeper…and Christ will give you light.* (Ephesians 5:14)

But, what about second generation pansies? According to the book, if the flowers are left where they were planted until they go to seed, the seeds will be borne on the winds and dropped wherever the wind so desires. When they find fertile ground, there they will remain lifeless until the next growing season. Most will not germinate, but against all expectation, when the *sun* returns, warm and nourishing, some do germinate—and *Voila!* New life, ALL NEW blossoms—blooming where they are planted, because…

"When you put a seed into the ground, it doesn't grow into a plant unless it dies first…then God gives it a new body—just the kind He wants it to have." (1 Corinthians 15:36-38 NLT); "The truth is, a kernel (seed) must be planted in the soil. Unless it dies it will be alone—just a single (lifeless) seed. But its death will produce many new seeds—a plentiful harvest of new seeds." (John 12:24 NLT) Jesus had much to say about our need to "die to self," take up our cross and follow Him. (See Matthew 16:24)

Dear Lord, Let my seed die so that Your seed may live…help me to have faith to produce *Your* harvest. May I always trust you to grow me—bountifully. Please help me to see all the beautiful pictures of "a life in Christ" in this real life parable. Help me to live out more of them, to allow the wind of the Holy Spirit to pick me up and place me where you want me—and then to do all I can do to bloom where you plant me. Amen.

Am I...Are you—really blooming where we've been planted? Traditionally, a pansy stands for *Thoughts and Remembrance*. . .Will our fruit last—will it remain? *"I have chosen you that you should bear fruit... fruit that will last."* (Jesus speaking in John 15:16.)

Do others see the beauty and fragrance of Christ in us—now? Will our plantings spring up and continue to be a blessing when we are no longer here?

Am I living my life with that in mind?
What will my spiritual legacy be?

"Jesus invites us to outlive our lives, not just in heaven but here on earth...A salute to long life: goodness that outlives the grave, love that outlives the final breath...May you live in such a way that your death is just the beginning of your life."[7]

"The greatest use of life is to spend it for something that will outlast it."
William James—Psychologist and Philospher.

---

7   Max Lucado in <u>*Outlive Your Life*</u> (Thomas Nelson Publishers)

A Summer Treat—Taste and See

Remember the Nat King Cole song (1963) "Those Lazy, Hazy, Crazy Days of Summer"? It implies that summer is a more "laid back" season with more free time...It does seem that folks read more often in summer.—It's not unusual to hear, "That's going to be my first *summer read* this year", often referring to one of the latest books on the *New York Times best seller list*...titles such as THE SHACK or THE HARBINGER...

There are several I'd like to recommend for your summer's read this year; there is one, however, on *God's* list of "essentials" all year 'round. It's a real love letter...with mystery, adventure, intrigue, poetry, life-giving formulas and more...

The Epistle of Paul the Apostle to the Romans

Take a new look at this old classic...Hear Martin Luther's critique of this literary giant: "This epistle is the chief part of the New Testament and the very purest gospel...it can never be read or pondered too much...The more it is dealt with, the more precious it becomes and ***the better it tastes.***"

Many scholars believe it to be the most complete account of God's plan of salvation—all we need to know on the doctrine of salvation...I also see it as an excellent source when we want to explain *why* we believe—*what* we believe.

I recently had the refreshing experience of reading Romans in the paraphrased version *The Message*. Translator Eugene Peterson in his introduction to the book says in part: "The letter to the Romans is a piece of exuberant and passionate thinking...Paul takes logic and argument, poetry and imagination, Scripture and prayer, creation, history and experience, and weaves them all into this letter that has become the premier document of Christian theology."

I'd like to recommend reading at least chapters 14 and 15 in a modern language version.

Back in the 1970's—a *cutesy* gospel song asked, "If you were arrested for being a Christian, would there be enough evidence to convict you?" I think that was the question in Paul's mind as he wrote... Listen to the way he presents his case as if he were in a court of law submitting evidence to prove the truth. Paul shows that before God, we are all guilty of sin—and then he tells us that God himself provided the absolution...Jesus Christ became our propitiation, securing our salvation with His shed blood. He goes on to point us beyond salvation to a victorious Christian life through the power of the Holy Spirit. Apparently he wanted to be sure the church developed an unwavering grasp of the truth concerning the gospel of Christ.

Paul exhorts us to not use our new-found liberty for "license"; to be an example, not a stumbling block; to be encouragers, and affirmers—to love—unconditionally. He expels today's theories...*if it feels good, it must be good...you only have to please yourself...I'm OK, you're OK, etc.* Paul would label that *as just so much trash!*

He tells us we must place our life in God's hands, and just "let go and let God." Hear these words: *"God helping you; take your everyday ordinary life—your sleeping, eating, going-to-work, and walking around life—and place it before God as an offering."* (Romans 12:1 MSG)

We have barely touched on the essentials to the Christian life covered in this love letter from God...*O taste and see that the Lord is good; blessed is the man who trusts Him.* (Psalm 34:8 NKJV)

The table is set, the feast is ready—but you must TASTE for yourself!

**The only part of the Word that will work
for you is the part you *know*...
You can only *know* the parts you frequently consume.**

Rooted and Built up

In the latter part of June, a pastor friend stopped by to chat with Bill and me. He admired Bill's flourishing little 8x16 foot tomato garden in the back of the garage—large, dark-green, leafy plants hanging with fruit.

As we returned to the house, he commented on my herb garden which adorns our deck with greenery and tantalizing, savory aromas. I drew his attention to the difference between one of the potted herbs on the deck and one in the tomato garden—the identical starter plant, transplanted at the same time, and tended with the same loving care. But, those planted directly in the ground were much larger, greener, and appeared much stronger. Well…my friend's insight was a lesson from heaven…

"For a plant to become really strong," he said, "strong enough to withstand all the shocks it's apt to receive from the elements of nature, its roots must be able to go down very deep—once they get down deep, they need space to begin to spread—to *reach out*; this gives the plant balance and stability."

It didn't take me long to make that scripture analogy! It caused me to ponder—in the light of God's Kingdom, am I satisfied to be a *potted plant* or do I desire to be a strong deeply-rooted *in Christ plant?* A potted plant does well for a time, but with insufficient depth and space, it becomes root bound, and plant lovers know what that requires…repotting… pruning and trimming—nearly starting all over again—or it dries up and dies! As Christians, we must allow God to constantly prune, trim, and place us in the proper sized vessel, according to our growth in Him, so our roots become deeper and stronger.

I recall the difference between the steady, slow-growing, deeply-rooted, mighty oak tree and the faster-growing tall pines we once had in our yard—the roots of the huge pines were so shallow, they were partially visible above the ground. One summer when a fierce windstorm came, in one quick SWOOSH the tallest pine was toppled, roots attached! The oak next to it stood strong and vigorous.

Do our roots go deep into Christ's love, forgiveness and grace? Have we relinquished our space to His will, and given Him room to develop our roots—allowing them to go deep and spread out...reaching, ever reaching to produce even more fruit? Do we tend them daily with the food and water of the Word—and encourage new growth and direction through prayer and communion? If so, we will gain the strength and stability required to withstand whatever elements of life God may allow to come our way...*Let your roots grow down into Him and draw up nourishment from Him, so you will grow in faith, strong and vigorous in the truth you were taught. (*Colossians 2:7 NLT)

"The Scriptures clearly teach...The principle of fruit-bearing is a 'life-principle.' Life develops from a life-source; it cannot be manufactured. Fruit is not made—it grows as the requirements of the life-principle are met. In contrast, the works of the flesh are described in Scriptures as a negative result of human effort, without the Holy Spirit...The flesh can produce nothing but evil works while the Holy Spirit produces Christ-like fruit. The former requires self-effort and results in death; the latter requires obedience to the Holy Spirit and produces life and peace."[8]

*The Lord will guide you always; He will satisfy your needs in a sun-scorched land and will strengthen your frame. You will be like a well-watered garden, like a spring whose waters never fail. (*Isaiah 58:11)

Sunshine or rain—hailstorm or flood; He will walk us through—His grace will sustain us. We will be *"like trees planted along the riverbank, bearing fruit each season without fail. Their leaves will never wither, and in all things they will prosper."* (See Psalm 1:1-6 NLT)

---

8   Dr. Fuchsia Pickett, author and Bible teacher. Charisma Magazine, On-line, "Spirit-Led Woman," 5/9/2013

Let The Sunshine In

Heavenly sunshine, heavenly sunshine!
Flooding my soul with glory divine!
Heavenly sunshine, heavenly sunshine!
Hallelujah, Jesus is mine. (Unknown)

In recent years, we not only downsized our home, but also the garden…
As I see the lush and lovely tomato plants in Bill's little patch behind
the garage, I'm reminded of the large and beautiful gardens he had for
so many years—one in particular comes to mind—what a summer that
was for vegetable gardening. Bill had just retired and was enjoying his
garden more than ever. We were having an unusually warm, sunny
summer, with plenty of rain. For weeks now we had been feasting on
the incomparable taste of assorted veggies fresh from the garden. Our
mouths watered, anticipating the soon-to-be, ruby-red succulence of
the tomatoes just waiting to ripen.

The plants were so green and lush—like round, green hedges, nearly
weighted down with many "beef-steak tomatoes". By the end of July,
Bill was becoming concerned; they just didn't seem to be turning color
like they should and some even looked as if they might rot on the vine
while still green. He had trimmed away quite a few leaves near the bottom of the vines…The constant dampness, because the sun couldn't get
in there, had caused some mold. Some vines and fruit were withering,
in danger of rotting without enough sun. Finally realizing he needed
to take drastic action if we were to enjoy any of the fruit, he began to
prune some more—and some more, until they were mere skeletons of
the bushy green mounds they had been…Nearly unrecognizable had it
not been for all the tomatoes hanging on for dear life!

Now the light could get through, the sun's rays could encourage the
completion of the growth and ripening process—the master of the

garden would soon be gathering beautiful plump ripe fruit! Imagine the loss that might have been because the sun in all its glory could not get through the thick, *unnecessary* foliage. Oh, it looked green and lush, but where the sun doesn't penetrate, the fruit that began to grow cannot ripen, it rots instead.

Do you see the analogy? Do you ever feel as though the 'Son' is too far away—like you are just *hanging in limbo* spiritually? Turn to the Master Gardener—and hang on dear soul—accept the pruning and you will fulfill the Master's plan! Like a parent who disciplines his child because he loves them—God disciplines only those He loves!

God, our Master Gardener must sometimes drastically prune us—when we take on too much foliage, no matter how good it may look, or how right it may seem to us—sometimes there is just too much "me," and that blocks out the "light of the Son." So, we are in danger of becoming unfruitful. Anything we allow to come between us and the light of God's Word or the refreshing water of the Spirit, will cause a lack of fruit—or a decaying of the fruit that had begun to form.

It is important to remember we live in a sin-sick world, so we will inevitably be faced with trials and tribulations—this doesn't mean God causes them. However, He often allows them; these, too, are pruning, but always remember—the pruning tool is being yielded under the watchful eye of a gracious loving God. He also prunes us in good times—testing and enabling our fruit to thrive and multiply.

"The fruit of the Spirit is love, joy, peace, patience, kindness, goodness, faithfulness, gentleness and self-control." (Galatians 5:22) *"I am the true vine and my Father is the gardener. He cuts off every branch that doesn't produce fruit, and He prunes the branches that do bear fruit so they will bear even more."* (John 15:1-2 NLT)…

If we recognize His hand of love, He will always help us through and draw us closer to Him and His Word…He works in any and all circumstances to show us the way to peace, joy and fruitful abundance in Him.

If we have fellowship with God, we won't be stumbling around in darkness…God is pure light and there is no trace of darkness in Him…so if we walk in "The Light", we experience a shared life with Him and one another. (Taken from 1 John 1:5-7 MSG)

"Suffering times are a Christian's harvest times."
(Charles H. Spurgeon)

Hear the Daisies of the Field

"Daisies don't tell," oh, but they do.
She says much about life if you listen.
In tones of velvety white, her petals shimmer
Like tiny feathers of silken ivory,
They grip the small golden orb that holds life,
Soft yet firm and blazing yellow—
Like the very sun from which she draws strength.

She often stands with grace
Amongst a field of weeds
In elegant simplicity—all the while knowing
She is at the mercy of those
Who would try to pluck her,
Use her, waste her...
"She loves me, she loves me not..."

Still she dances gaily as the breezes will,
Hanging on, aware that one day soon
Her life-giving center will become
Hard and dry—the yellow drab,
Unyielding and lifeless,
Strength vanquished,
No longer sustaining her beauty.

One by one, each petal succumbs
And falls like winter snow.
Her stem will now wither and die—
And yet there remains the seed
As it falls to the ground,
She will bloom again—resurrected!
The planting of the Lord...

Beauty from the Storm

[They] will blossom like a Lily. Like a cedar of Lebanon they shall send down their roots; their beauty will be like an olive tree, their fragrance like the cedars of Lebanon. (Hosea 14:6)

It was early evening; I sat by the back patio door watching the torrent of August rain pummeling down. I knew the ground needed it, yet I wanted to chant like I did as a youngster, "Rain, rain, go away; come again another day." My beautiful double impatiens had reached that ravishing stage—deep pinks, full and flowing with grandeur. Or they had been. As the deluge beat down on them, they became limp and bent over, touching their storm-battered heads to the ground. I could almost feel the pain of it all. I was sure they would never come back to full beauty anymore this season. I couldn't watch any longer—I made myself busy far from the glass door.

Soon the storm subsided. I looked out to see the sun come out bright and warm, producing a glorious rainbow stretching across the deep rose-colored sunset. The next morning I stepped out the front door and was greeted by a vernal fragrance—like laundry just off the clothesline on a sunny, spring day. Hesitantly, I rounded the corner of the house to check my flowers...what a glorious surprise! They looked brighter and stronger than before the storm, standing straight and strong as though reaching for the heavens. And I realized...the rain had soaked the soil, which began to send much-needed nutrients to the stems—which in turn fed the blossoms. What a lesson!

That's the way it is with the storms of life...difficult to endure; even more difficult to watch someone we love endure. Often storms are potentially destructive—and yet our loving heavenly Father knows just what we need, and when, and how much. He allows the storms, indeed sometimes sends them. And He alone can take the devastation and turn it into a thing of beauty. I pray that from now on, whenever I find myself in the midst of one of life's threatening squalls, I will by His grace endure with patience; realizing when the storm is over, I can be found in the grace and beauty of the Lord—stronger, wiser and ready to bloom, even more graciously.

Lord, you have been a shelter from the storm...Isaiah 25:4

Joy Comes in the Morning

So often thru our trials and tears
We don't seem to understand,
God's still at work just being God,
Though we don't see His hand…

Breaking, melting, molding, shaping,
Then putting to the fire,
Our lives, our hopes, our hidden dreams
Our every deep desire.

Hear Him say, "Hold on my child
Though tears must fall tonight,
The morn will once again bring joy;
Your God does all things right."

Just as the showers attending a storm
Will oft contain a rainbow,
The tears that come with every trial,
Will bring to our life a new glow.

We'll find our glistening tear-brimmed eyes
Will bring into focus, His plan…
Beauty for ashes, and joy for mourning,
He Who is Faithful—the **"Great *I AM"*.**

*"Let the morning bring me word of your unfailing love
for I have put my trust in you. Show me the way I
should go, for to you I lift up my soul."*
—Psalm 143:8

Take the Plunge!

The Good ole summertime—gardens, picnics, camping, and *swimming*—in the beautiful, though often chilly lakes and rivers of Northern Wisconsin. Oh, what youthful memories that conjures up! I always looked forward to that part of summer. When we were young, from June right up to the "dog days" of August; with hot sun-drenched bodies, we headed nearly every day for Hodag Beach. That first dip was always difficult, so as youngsters we would just plunge in...and tauntingly call to those still struggling to get wet, "Come on in, Sissy!"

As my summers began to pile on the years, I wasn't always quite so brave...With a bit of apprehension, I stepped in *ankle deep*, and stood there shivering for a moment, while the toddlers with their sand pails and shovels look up quizzically. Can you identify with me?

Cautiously you take the next step, still not anxious to go all the way; dubiously you continue on and soon you're *knee-deep*. It's not getting much warmer, but you can't just stand there, so on you go, now taking strong, more determined steps, as your body must tread more and more water—then it happens—suddenly!—the icy water pierces your waist with a shocking jolt, like a band of hard, cold steel! For a moment it takes your breath away, and your first instinct is to turn and head back to shore; but you realize—if you're going to *swim*, you MUST GO DEEPER! So, you take the plunge and—oh, how invigorating! It feels much warmer once you plunge in—what a sweet sense of *surrender*, and yet, one of empowerment! And you wonder, "Why did I struggle so?"

This always reminds me of Ezekiel's vision of the river of God (Ezekiel 47:1-5). It flowed out of the temple of God and covered the entire land. Ezekiel is encouraged to step in, and soon finds himself standing in water up *to his ankles*...then *knee-deep*, yet another step and he is *waist deep*...There Ezekiel says, *"The river was too deep to cross without swimming."* (Verse 5 NLT)

That river represents several things, including the promise that the Holy Spirit's influence will grow deeper and stronger in the world throughout history until it covers the whole earth. Ezekiel is painting us a picture of ourselves...As we walk steadily deeper into the river of spiritual life, we come to a point where we cannot stand against the current in our own strength...We must swim and go increasingly deeper *in the waters of the Holy Spirit, releasing ourselves entirely to Him.* There is no need to fear—He is our comforter and guide—and always a Gentleman. Read on through verse 12 to see the many benefits of fruitfulness to be experienced on both banks of the river—if we are willing to "take the plunge".

In John 7:37-39, we find the same invitation from Jesus Himself—to come to the river of living water. (He is referring to the Holy Spirit.)... He invites us to *come thirsty – come often – drink deeply*—to plunge in and be refreshed and satisfied—and we will in turn become channels of refreshment to others.

Let's always remember, the shallow shoreline is for youngsters who are still contented to sit and build *castles in the* sand—ankle deep... is for children who can't swim. Knee-deep, you might be inclined to sit down and just let the water flow around you—enjoying that gentle "touchy-feel-y" brush with the water of the Spirit—but if you remain there, you will be lulled into a false sense of satisfaction—going nowhere—never knowing the refreshing power nor the thrilling benefits of swimming the waters of the Holy Spirit.

I really like the way J. Lee Grady put it...

"Many of us get stuck at this point. God calls us to total surrender, but we either turn back or park ourselves in perpetual limbo. We are either paralyzed by fear of losing control or we stubbornly refuse to jettison the things that will sink us... The best thing we can do is dive in at this stage...We must let go and allow His swift current to take us where He wants us...It's the best place to be, but no one is going to throw us into His river against our will."[9]

---

9   The Holy Spirit is not for Sale, Chosen Books; 2010; by J. Lee Grady

Virginia Phillips Kreft

Now you have a decision to make—this is a crucial point—you've come half way—do you swim or turn back to shore? Why not accept Jesus' invitation to trust Him…and plunge in!

If you allow the living water of God's Spirit to touch you and flow out of you, it will bring healing and abundant fruitfulness. (Ezekiel 47:12; John 7: 38)

Notice what Ezekiel said with each step of his journey into the river: *"He led me..."* If you'll take that first step in your *river journey,* you will soon realize—Jesus is there all along the way—loving, encouraging, leading…never pushing.

Have you ventured in? Are you moving on? Are you ready to take the plunge?

**"Plunge in today and be made complete,
Glory to His name!"[10]**

---

10   Hymn by Elisha A. Hoffman, John H. Stockton; 1878

Come To the Waters

Why are you downcast and weary my soul?
Why so disturbed within me?
I will hope in my God and I shall be whole,
My Savior, my God, I will praise Thee.

Just as the deer pants for streams of cool water,
So pants my soul for you, Lord.
My soul longs to drink of your pure living water,
I come ever trusting Your Word—

"O, come, my child, I know you are thirsty,"
Thus calls the Lord God Almighty,
"I will pour water on him who comes thirsty
And drench the parched ground that assails thee.

On all those who come I will pour out my blessing,
I will write My Name on your hand,
The Alpha, Omega, your King, your Redeemer
Great God—One and Only—I AM!"

—Inspired by Psalm 42; Isaiah 44:3-7

This Is the Refreshing

This is the rest with which You may cause the weary to rest…this is the refreshing." (Isaiah 28:12 NKJV)

Once again it is here…the hot, humid, and sometimes harried days of July and August. Welcome as it is—it also means sweltering, tedious chores of all sorts. Lawn mowing, trimming the hedge, weeding the garden, painting the house. Or just out for a morning run, enjoying a friendly tennis match, shooting baskets, playing catch…In the heat of the day, they all become tediously depleting. Don't you often reach the point where you wonder how you can go on without a nice, cold drink?

How fortunate when someone who cares appears with a tall, frosty glass of lemonade or iced tea, maybe a Coke, or even better…crystal clear ice water! You hear the ice subtly tinkling in the glass, see the cool, sparkling jewel-like beads trickling down the side—instantly you put it to your lips and drink *deeply*. As it slakes your parched throat, the refreshing elixir seems to permeate every fiber of your body. With both hands you hold the cooling balm to your cheeks, then your burning brow—the back of your neck. It cools your being inside and out. You are once more refreshed indeed and able to continue…Ever so grateful for the thoughtfulness of the one who brought you refreshment. (At times we may have to call for someone because our otherwise willing "refresher" may not know our need until we ask!)

This word picture provides an important spiritual life application… Many of us are sometimes weary, discouraged, even overwhelmed by the toils of everyday circumstances, as well as unusual trials and afflictions; and we need someone who cares to come alongside with a word of refreshing…an offer to pray, to help—or just listen. Often it's someone who themselves have been discouraged and received refreshing from a friend. We need to be ready to be the refresher as well as the one in need of refreshing.

God uses people to refresh people!

The Apostle Paul was often in need of personal refreshing...In 2 Corinthians 7:5-7, he speaks of *no rest, harassed at every turn, conflicts on the outside, and fear inside... "but—God who encourages those who are discouraged, encouraged us by the arrival of Titus...his presence was a joy... and an encouragement..."* Notice, God didn't send an angel to refresh Paul; He sent Titus--a friend, who by his refreshing spirit, was able to refresh Paul.

Paul also asked God to bless the whole family of a certain believer named Onesiphorus because, *"He often refreshed me...he searched hard for me until he found me." (2 Timothy 1:16)... Of three others who came to him in Ephesus from the church in Corinth,* Paul states: *"They refreshed my spirit...such men deserve recognition." (I Corinthians 16:18) "Your love has given me great joy and encouragement, because you have refreshed the hearts of the saints."* (Philemon 7)

Dave Wilkerson exhorts..."The ministry of refreshing clearly includes seeking out those who are hurting. We hear a lot about power in the church these days... I say there is great healing power that flows out of a refreshed and renewed person...There are people who need you, and the Lord intends your past consolations to bring refreshing to them."[11]

Friends, might our words be a cooling hand on someone's feverish brow today? A soothing balm for someone's wound...A cheerful ray of sunlight and friendship to someone's lonely existence? Do it now—don't wait until you "have the time," that may be too late. You don't want to miss any of the Lord's sacred appointments.

"...It is like precious oil poured on the head...like dew...there the Lord bestows His blessing, even life forever more." (From Psalm 133)

---

11   ¹David Wilkerson Newsletter, May 6, 2006—World Challenge Inc.

Annual Church Picnic

It's a sunny-Sunday afternoon on the waterfront in beautiful Hodag Park. The church family gathers joyously with all the warm and loving ambience of a big family reunion…Games, baseball, boating, visiting, reminiscing, singing—AND FOOD! So much—so delectable! Every family brings a main dish to pass and a dessert or side salad. Barring none, the most special picnic of the year is our annual church picnic… one of my favorite church activities—and one of the last for the summer. I can still remember the afterglow of last year. This year will be the same I'm sure—*a bunch of paupers around a banquet table "fit for a King"!* Table after table, full to overflowing—all there just for the taking… there is no reason for anyone to go away hungry…Come to the table—reach out—take. No matter what your favorites, there's bound to be something that pleases your taste.

And then the finishing touch—as the sun slowly begins its descent toward the horizon, bordered by tall pines, green hardwoods and the blue hues of Boom Lake…we all gather down at the lakeside for water baptisms…what solemn, blessed moments. We begin to raise our voices in praise and worship, as one by one, those being baptized walk slowly into the water—as an outward symbol of their inward commitment to follow their Lord and Savior, Jesus Christ. With glowing faces, each rises from the water renewed. And as the service closes in prayer, there is a feeling of wanting to "linger a while" sensing a holy-like presence…I remember thinking as I left last year, "This must be just a tiny little taste of what heaven will be like!"

Another Church Picnic

Our Northern Wisconsin summers are so very beautiful, but a little short—and folks like to take advantage, so most any reason is a good excuse for a picnic or cook-out, particularly at one of the many beautiful lakesides and riverbanks. None are quite as special as the annual August event—but the fun and fellowship are equal. For instance, this year there was a new picnic celebration—announced in the bulletin the week before, the **"End of School" Picnic—June 7, 4—6 PM at Hodag Park—bring your own picnic lunch"**. Many came and enjoyed…I suspect some who weren't really prepared still tasted of the Lord's graciousness…might you have been one of those?

You forgot all about it until you were on your way home from work that day… "Maybe I won't go" you thought; "I know I don't have anything to pack in a lunch, but I told the Pastor I'd be there." It's already 5:30, no time to stop and shop, so you decide to just drive through the fast food place on the way and get a sandwich and a Coke, that's enough. "I won't stay long anyway—at least I'll be showing up." Just before getting to the order window, you remember, you only have two $1.00 bills and some change for cash—and no checkbook or debit card…thank God for dollar menus!

When you arrive, almost everyone is already seated. A family you only know by name is all together at one table—"Mom" sees you and invites you to sit down to eat with them. That picnic table was lined from one end to the other with a FEAST! That Mom had apparently worked all day cooking and baking…she had quite a family to feed—three in elementary school, two in middle school, one just graduated—this was a special celebration, and she meant to serve a meal to match it! From chicken to apple pie and everything to go with it! Several times the mom says, "Please help yourself, I made way too much." "Oh no, I couldn't," you reply, embarrassed… "I'm not really all that hungry; I'll just enjoy my sandwich." You sit there sipping your drink, staring at the foil wrapped "dinner" in front of you—longing for something more… asking yourself why you didn't give it more time and importance—but, you made your stupid decision and you have to live with it! *It's all too ridiculous to be real, isn't it?*

And then the *"piece de' resistance"*…the oldest boy—the high school graduate said, "Please, would you consider trading me this chicken for your hamburger? We have chicken all the time and that is one of my favorite kind of burgers." And he passed you his whole plate—including the fork and knife! You came feeling like an orphan—and you're eating like one of the family.

I can't help thinking—that's how we often respond to the banquet table God has prepared for us every hour of every day—any time, any place… with Christ as Host! David talks about it in the beloved 23rd Psalm: *"You prepare a feast for me in the presence of my enemies."* (Psalm 23:5). I think sometimes the *worst enemy* keeping us from partaking fully of that feast is ourselves. We pass by *on the go* and grab a little snack, and hurry away, mumbling, I'll "fill up" later; but later we're still caught up with "things". Running late, we once again grab some "fast food", telling ourselves, "I don't have time now—this will have to hold me; I'll get a real meal later." All the time you're ignoring the fact that your whole being is groaning with hunger pangs—how sad. The worst of it is—*"later"* seldom arrives…and we continue to just eat *on the run* from Sunday to Sunday—never enjoying the banquet Jesus is waiting to share with us—daily!

So we stumble along, too busy, too hurried—looking for the right answers in all the wrong places. Hoping to partake of some spiritual "nugget" handed down from some of the *fast food teachers* along the way—the sugary sweets and empty calories served up by some TV Evangelist or a "three minute" daily devotional…anything "quick and to the point" that we can pick up when we have a minute to spare…We hardly notice we are never fully satisfied, close to becoming malnourished—all because we won't take enough time for the feast prepared right here in our own home—at His banquet table—prepared by Him; flowing with the spirit-building nourishment of the Word—and the life-giving power of praise and worship. The Psalmist, after lifting his heart in love and adoration, declares: *"You have made me as strong as a wild bull, how refreshed I am by your power."* Sounds like he's been to the banquet table!

You know, if we will make time to satiate ourselves at His table, God will even supply take outs to carry us through the day! There is no charge—the price has been paid, and there is <u>no tax</u> and <u>no tip</u> required! We need only show-up and dig in!

I wonder that God doesn't weary of our self-induced, anorexic, spiritual malnourishment, but He doesn't—Instead He waits patiently, saying— *Here I am! I stand at the door and knock, if anyone hears my voice and opens the door, I will come in and eat with Him, and He with me.* (Revelation 3:20) You know, of course—that is written NOT to unbelievers, but to the church, to you and me! Jesus wants us to partake of a banquet—WITH HIM—DAILY!

Jesus is saying, "Please, give me that sandwich—don't settle for that same old McMuffin or $1.00 hamburger, you need more than that— come, sup with me." He wants to be our *all in all*—but we keep moving frantically through life without a proper diet, picking up a snack here and there...growing weaker and wondering why.

Do you know anyone like that—spiritually? So hungry for real nourish-ment...stumbling along, hanging on for dear life—But not willing to make the time to sit for a while at the banquet table where the Lord is waiting to dine with them.

You know, it isn't that God really wants our sandwich—but He would like us to surrender it—in trade for all that's prepared for us at His banquet table—His DAILY BREAD!

> *Jesus said, "I am the bread of life, he who comes to*
> *me will never go hungry..."* —John 6:35
> *...Wonderful times of refreshment will come from the presence of the Lord.*
> —Acts 3:20 NLT

Life-giving Aroma Therapy

I come to the garden alone—and the joy we share...

I have noticed the hotter and more humid the summer weather, the richer and more intense is the fragrance of summer foliage. We have a small but lovely 8x12 foot patio surrounded by lush shrubs and hanging baskets. Each day, I like to step out to my little patio early in the morning, coffee in hand—*while the dew is still on the roses!* With the shrubs flowering and my hanging baskets in full bloom—the strong fragrance emanating throughout that small space virtually fills up my senses. I just want to stay there, soaking it in, letting the sweet aroma seemingly penetrate every fiber of my being. When I finally step back inside to my daily routine, the essence seems to remain in my nostrils like a vapor, putting a spring in my step and a song in my heart.

In the evening as I go out to water the source of the fragrant beauty, Bill often joins me. While the sun slips below the horizon and the dew point begins to climb, he also senses the same scintillating savor wafting across our patio. It is not always quite as permeating as morning, still—very uplifting...prompting expressions of gratitude and thankfulness for the blessing of such *simple* pleasures. And I'm reminded of a favorite scripture ...

2 Corinthians 2:14-16: *"Thanks be to God, who always leads us in triumphal procession in Christ, and <u>through us spreads everywhere</u> the fragrance of the knowledge of Him. For we are to God the fragrance of Christ among those who are being saved and among those who are perishing. To the one we are the smell of death, to the other, the fragrance of life. And who is equal to such a task?"* Yes, who indeed! What an awesome responsibility! Thank God we can say as Paul said, *"Yet not I—but Christ..."*

If we are to be the *fragrance* of Christ, we must take time in His presence, up close and personal, soaking up His beauty and sweet savor.

"Let the beauty of the Lord our God be upon us...
*and establish the work of our hands." (*Psalm 90:17 NKJV)

Lily Of The Valley, let your sweet aroma fill my life—with the
sweet fragrance of Your presence,
And let it draw others to You and You only.

"And He walks with me and He talks with me,
And He tells me I am His own,
And the joy we share, as we tarry there,
None other has ever known."

On the Jericho Road

Who do you most identify with in the familiar Bible story—Jesus' parable of the "Good Samaritan"? Even the more secular of our society frequently use the term to describe someone who does a "good deed" for a stranger. But how often do we see ourselves as the one lying wounded on the side of the road?

"A Jewish man was travelling on a trip from Jerusalem to Jericho, and he was attacked by bandits."—so the story begins in Luke 10:30-37 NLT…along the road he is robbed, stripped of his clothes, severely beaten and left on the roadside to die.

"By chance a Jewish Priest came along; but when he saw the man lying there, he crossed to the other side of the road and passed him by. A temple assistant walked over and looked at him lying there but he also passed him by on the other side."

These fine, upstanding citizens came by, walked over and looked—and turned a deaf ear and a blind eye to the man's groans of pain and bleeding wounds—and passed by *condescendingly* on the opposite side of the road.

Soon another figure appears—a stranger, an alien, of meek and lowly ancestry. *"And when he saw the man, he felt deep pity"*….He gently and caringly bathes the man's wounds, offers him a drink—and lifts him up and transports him to a place of care and healing.

I'm sure we have each experienced a spiritual Jericho Road—all similar, yet different—Who is this one who shows up on *our* desolate Jericho Road? Who is this unlikely rescuer who walks with us in the valley of the shadow of death? He sees our need; even sees our invisible wounds when others don't seem to have time to look closely.

He is none other, of course, than the Lord Jesus Christ—our Good Samaritan. He says, *"Take my yoke upon you, and learn of me; for I am meek and lowly of heart, and you shall find rest for your souls. For my yoke is easy, and my burden is light."* (Matthew 11:29-30 KJV)

What sort of robber has waylaid you—Pain, loss, loneliness, binding bad habits, unconfessed sin? Are you struggling physically, emotionally, financially...perhaps spiritually? Are you feeling lost, abandoned, wounded, broken, unwanted?

Whatever your need, call on Him, He will be there—He will not pass you by. Even when all your strength is gone...He will hear even the faintest cry of your heart. He has promised, *"I will never leave you or forsake you."* (Hebrews 13:5 NKJV) *"He heals the brokenhearted and binds up their wounds."* (Psalm 147:3)

Often, we will not be the one wounded, but the one the Holy Spirit calls to "come alongside" and help the wounded one to the place of healing—to shelter in the arms of God...Let's pray that God will help us stay in touch and be sensitive to His Spirit for just such opportunities—don't miss the Sacred Appointment waiting for you—whether you are the hurting—or the one called to help the hurting.

"Assuredly, when you did it to one of the least of these my brothers and sisters, you were doing it for me." (Matthew 25:40)

Higher Ground

Our Father who is in heaven...lead me not into
temptation, but deliver me from the evil one..."
(The Lord's Prayer – Matthew 6:13)

"I want to live above the world, tho' Satan's darts at me are hurled;
For faith has caught the joyful sound, the song of saints on higher ground.
My heart has no desire to stay, where doubts arise and fears dismay;
Tho' some may dwell where these abound, My
prayer, my aim is higher ground."[1]

Lord, I know not where the path will lead,
Whether smooth and level or rocky and steep,
I do not know how far it reaches—
Through deep dark forest, or along sandy beaches.

I do know, Lord, I'll make it through,
For each step I take I'll take with You;
Holding your hand, I'm heavenward bound,
Lord, lead me on to higher ground.

"Lord, lift me up and let me stand
By faith on heaven's table land;
A higher plane than I have found—
Lord, plant my feet on higher ground."[12]

And now, all glory to God, who is able to keep you from stumbling, and who
will bring you into His glorious presence innocent of sin and with great joy.
Jude 24

---

12   Johnson Oatman, Jr. 1856-1922

~~~~~~~

Autumn

A time of Reverie

A Time of Transition

~~~~~~~

Autumn Introspection

"There is a time for everything, and a season for everything under heaven." —Ecclesiastes 3:1

I like all the seasons, but autumn is my favorite. There's a feel about it, a unique and hard-to-miss ambience in the air. (All the more, if you're from Wisconsin—and a Packer fan!) Of course, my love of autumn is more entrenched than that—the leaves are a great part of it. What an array of majestic artistry! And the silvery, crisp-frosted mornings—a refreshing change from summer. There's even a welcome return to routine as vacations are over—school begins.

The firewood is cut; there are pumpkins *everywhere.* And oh, the aromas that fill the air...Smoldering leaves, hot apple cider...Then along comes Thanksgiving Day; a time to pause and remember that God has indeed blessed us abundantly, so we offer a time of specific reflection and thanks-giving.

Yes, autumn is (or should be) a season of reflection. Gaining new perspective as we take a stroll along the back roads of our mind; thinking about the *what–where and why*—evaluating the way we were, and verifying the way we want to be.

This implies change—*transition*...The foliage changes, the weather changes, even the time changes from Daylight Saving back to Central Standard Time... Birds make their annual southward flight; squirrels finish storing acorns; salmon start their phenomenal swim back to the spawning grounds. A long winter's nap is in store for some of the animals. All these creatures of the natural world follow their individual agendas without any external instruction.

So it is with our life in Christ—at any time He deems right, He gently, quietly and lovingly moves within our lives, taking us into autumn, a spiritual season of transition—when He inscrutably writes *His* agenda on the tablets of our hearts and waits—patiently, graciously, on the sidelines—for us to accept the challenge *He* has set before us. Will we accept—*naturally?* Will we comply—*spiritually?* If so, let's grasp His hand and hold on tenaciously as we walk on into our autumn—for surely, winter won't be far behind! But fret not—no matter how harsh it gets, He will be there also! He is everywhere His grace is welcomed.

> *"Since we live by the Spirit, let us keep in step with the Spirit."*
> —Galatians 5:25

Bring to the Storehouse

We looked out the patio door just in time to see a silver streak cross the walkway. Soon the furry flash went by in the opposite direction—a grey squirrel, of course. After several such round trips, we took up our watch outside. Our little friend would emerge from the wooded area on the far north end of the complex—come scurrying past all the way to the wooded area on the south end. *Back and forth, forth and back*—He was undoubtedly storing fodder for winter. Foraging diligently, he made each trip to his *storage shed* steady and deliberate. However, as he made each trip back, he would stop along the way, attentively stand on his hind legs and take in the sights and sounds around him…Our presence only a few steps away didn't deter him at all!

Yes, *the **sights, sounds,** and **smells*** of the fall season are here—a season of preparation for the winter to follow. I do look forward to cooler days and the return to routine…School begins, clocks fall back…and football—go Packers! I profoundly enjoy **the sights**—leaves of hardwoods turning from green to orange, the bright scarlet of the maples, the copper plating on the oak leaves…Harvested pumpkins making their annual appearance, lined up against doors and walls everywhere; many on bales of straw with Mr. Scarecrow standing watch…Firewood piles climbing higher and higher—and school buses…Hear **the sounds**—in crisp clearness, reverberating the life all around us on a frosty morning…Dry leaves crackling underfoot—geese noisily honking overhead as they make their way south, and school children laughing cheerfully as they skip their way home together…Breathe in—**the smells**…the heady aroma of smoldering leaves—of wood smoke billowing from a nearby chimney—and simmering pots of cinnamon spiced apple cider…

We all welcome the transition of winter into spring—spring into summer…and then autumn. If only we could hold on to it longer—it seems the change from summer to autumn comes too quickly—and passes even more quickly. Each day reminding us winter is soon upon us and we want to be ready! And so it is with the seasons of the soul and spirit. Have you built a spiritual storehouse—a root-cellar—deep in the love of Jesus? Just Sunday Church won't do it, my friend—that's the frosting on the cake.

Each of us will face some austere times in our life. Jesus said: *"In this world you will have trouble..."* (John 16:33) He also said: *"Where your heart is, there your treasure will be also."* (Matthew 6:19-21) Are you storing up treasures in Christ to carry you through the less fruitful days, the more barren days of the winter of your soul? Are you prepared...wrapped in the blanket of His love, warmed by the fires of His Spirit?

God said, *"You will seek me and find me when you search for me with all your heart."* (Jeremiah 29:13) But...**It's much more difficult to find the acorns after the snows have fallen.**

The winter of the soul can appear when you least expect it...So replenish the storehouse—daily. And like the squirrel, be sure to enjoy the sights and sounds of God's presence along the way.

Lord, teach me to be more in attendance to Your Presence.

Romping

Bright Fall days were meant for walking,
Leaving the rake fixed soundly in the sod,
Off into the woods I went
To be alone with God.

My mind plays games of reminiscing,
Beneath my feet leaves snap, crackle, pop,
In my ear the cadence resounds,
And thoughts of younger days won't stop.

On the ground now, tumbling, giggling,
Then lying still in the filtering sun,
I listen…and I hear Him say,
Now didn't we have fun?

"…unless you change and become like little children,
you will never see the kingdom of heaven."
—Matthew 18:3

Stop, Drop, and Roll

It happens every year, everywhere in the country, as summer ends and fall begins...It's Back to School Time. The K–12 kids are all excited about another new school year, rejoining old friends not seen all summer, new clothes, new friends, new teacher, and new and lofty aspirations!

For most kids (including this one), some of the most enjoyable school days were the special visitor days...Often they were the community *Heroes and Helpers*...all with important information we were admonished to always remember—in order to keep safe, healthy—honest, trustworthy, etc. One of the earliest each year is often the observance of Fire Prevention Week. Do you recall the visit of your Friendly Fireman in his impressive looking uniform and bright hard hat?

Close your eyes and remember...The scenario he painted (when I was in grade school at least) was somewhat scary, but the response was fun to practice—*"Stop what you're doing, drop to the floor and—roll."* You would have thought some were auditioning for a school play—the boys screamed and fell over like they were one of the bad guys in a movie, the one who had just been shot by the good guy; the girls, of course, dropped daintily to their knees first, then gracefully eased themselves to the floor (so as not to crumple anything)and everyone began to roll... The reason for all this? If you are ever in a situation where your clothes are on fire, you have to act instinctively and immediately! There will be no time to think or to call someone...And the key to being prepared is to practice, practice, practice—STOP, DROP AND ROLL—STOP, DROP AND ROLL!

What we learned in elementary school could well be applied spiritually. We will all have occasion to use it—more than once in a lifetime—have we practiced enough—in the presence of God? Will we act instinctively when the searing flames of life situations engulf us?

I've been there, picture it…The fire is so very hot, the more I try to battle the flames, the hotter they become, and I'm thinking, "Dear God, will I survive this time?" And God's Word rings in my ears: *"Don't be surprised at the fiery trials you are going through, as if something strange were happening to you. Instead rejoice…so your faith though it is tested by fire may be proved genuine…"* (See 1 Peter 4:12-13 and 1:7-9) Nevertheless, I felt as if this fiery trial was going to consume me. Of course, I wasn't really on fire, but I was in the proverbial "fire of suffering" and it was painful. How could I be glad when I hurt so much? But, how could I be refined if I couldn't endure the test?

That's when the childhood lesson and the ensuing years of *practicing the Presence of God* should kick in…Though the fire we are in is a spiritual one, the response necessary to survive is much the same—don't run, don't whine, but…Stop, Drop and Roll…

Stop—running will be more dangerous, the fire will spread *even* faster, inflicting *even* deeper wounds. We must stop struggling against the bit.[13]

Drop—to our knees…assume a posture of awe before God; in reverence, and yes, even desperation; be honest—have a real talk with Jesus… we may hear ourselves saying something we didn't even realize was deep in our hearts. Here we find peace for our troubled souls and rest for our pummeled minds. When we drop to our knees, we are not accepting defeat or asking God to distinguish the flames before His appointed time. We are actually accepting, trusting, believing His love, grace and strength to save us from the inferno we're in. *"If we are thrown into the fiery furnace, the God we serve is able to save us." (Daniel 3:17)*

Roll-roll all your burdens and cares on Him (see 1 Peter 5:7). All our fears, pain and confusion; only He knows how to carry it. When we roll it over on Him, we realize why Peter could tell us to rejoice…The Lord's joy comes when we find His grace in suffering.

---

13   Read Psalm 32

Maybe it's time to stop running from the refiner's fire and let it purge you—by practicing this simple grade school teaching: STOP, DROP, and ROLL.

"These (fiery) trials are only to test your faith to show that it is strong and pure. It is being tested as fire tests and purifies gold—and your faith is far more precious to God than mere gold. So if your faith remains strong after being tried by fiery trials, it will bring you much praise and glory and <u>honor</u> on the day when Jesus Christ is revealed to the whole world…And <u>even now</u> you are happy with a glorious, inexpressible joy." (1 Peter 1:7-8 NLT)

It is joy unspeakable and full of glory and
the half has never yet been told…[14]

---

14   Hymn by Barney E. Warren, public domain

~~~~~~~

THANKSGIVING

~~~~~~~

Now I Lay Me Down to Sleep...

"It is a good thing to give thanks to the Lord.
And sing praises to Your name O Most High;
To declare Your lovingkindness in the morning
And Your faithfulness by night."
—Psalm 92:1-2

As I nestled my head in the pillow, I began to do as I like to most nights—make my last thoughts those of thankfulness to the Lord for His many blessings. Since I *(thankfully)* go to sleep very quickly, *I must confess,* I sometimes fall asleep in the middle of prayer! But—God understands! I usually stay awake at least long enough to quote (or sing) my favorite "going to sleep" scripture: *Bless the Lord O my soul and all that is within me, bless His holy name...*(See Psalm 103:1-5) On those rare occasions when my mind wants to keep racing, I pray: *"...I bring every thought into captivity to the obedience of Christ..."* (2 Corinthians 10:5 NKJV) Then I can settle in, all comfy and relaxed, and put myself to sleep with more songs of <u>praise</u>. (I don't usually like to make this a time for *petitions,* that has hopefully been acted on much earlier in the day.)

This night, my mind *was* quieted, yet I *wasn't* falling asleep...instead, joyous songs of thanks and praise kept bubbling up in my heart and spirit *spontaneously*! I sensed the Holy Spirit saying, "Hold fast to this moment—and share it." And so I shall...

At this holiday season, as you prepare to go to sleep, if you quote or sing simple praise from the very depth of your being...**you will find Thanksgiving and Christmas all tied up in one *beautiful gift of thanks and worship* to our Lord and Savior—Emmanuel.** If there's a concern about disturbing someone, sing and worship silently from your heart in jubilant silent crescendo, God hears it—He hears every cry of your heart! (A mute person can't verbalize out loud—yet He hears them and answers!) It could become a habit you'll want to continue all year! Here are a few suggestions to start, but create your own special medley.

Bless the Lord O my soul; Praise God from Whom All Blessings flow; More About Jesus; Take My Life and Let it Be; There's Something About That Name; Emmanuel; He is Lord; Majesty, Worship His Majesty; O, Come Let Us Adore Him.

O, YES, COME—ALL YE FAITHFUL—IN JOY and TRIUMPH!

God Bless—Sleep Well

Assorted Shades of Grace

My eyes blurred a little, wanting to tear, and I realized I was quietly gulping in an effort to swallow the lump in my throat—making it difficult to eat my dessert… It was exactly one week before Thanksgiving Day. The days approaching the Christmas holidays always put me in a very joyous mood—and I was, only…

Our monthly Red Hat Luncheon is always a time of gaiety. Sixteen of us "Red Hats of Grace" had gathered for our November fling at a local restaurant. From there, half of us headed to a lovely assisted-living facility to share with a few residents. What an enchanting sight! More than twenty of us all toll, gathered in their *parlor—a* huge circle of smiling faces, each topped off with a red hat! Nearly half of these glowing faces were residents (all elderly—a few with various levels of dementia), who had formed their own "in house" Red Hat Society. There they were all decked out in assorted Red Hat regalia…Once each month they meet around the table for refreshments and common bonding. In honor of our visit, they had made this their meeting day. We were there to share and have an old time sing-along, including a few Christmas Carols. Their joy was apparent as most of them sang out with gusto, *some even on key*! As I stopped singing to listen, I could hear a perfectly-pitched alto harmony. I had to ask—who? A hand immediately went up with a proud declaration of having sung in the church choir for years!

Soon we were gathered around their dining room tables for coffee and a luscious pumpkin dessert made by our ladies. I hadn't expected that dessert to bring this lump in my throat…but I recalled our last meeting and the sad event in between.

At our luncheon in October, as is often the practice of other Red Hatters, we decided to begin our meal with dessert—*this same pumpkin dessert.* We wanted to share this new recipe, and the restaurant had allowed us to bring in our own dessert and even provided the plates and forks. I recall our waitress not seeing the "fun" in our *dessert first* ritual, but then she was very young—and perhaps a little stressed out! Which reminded me about one paragraph in our own *original* Red Hats of Grace Creed—it states in part..."Adorned in our Red Hats and Purple attire, once each month we shall gather together for lunch and unadulterated fellowship and fun—*free of the cares and inhibitions that entangle the young*"...What a blessing!

No one was enjoying the entire process of *dessert first* more than Barb, who was seated directly across from me. As usual, she was the epitome of Red Hat Couture, always decked out in her purple outfits, complete with wild Red Hat, Boa, gloves and the works! I had first met Barb about ten years before when we partnered for a seniors' concert trip. She was quiet and soft-spoken, a delightful companion. About a year ago, Barb's husband had to be placed in a full nursing care facility; it was difficult for her. She had always been a little frail, still she had cared for him for years, but finally the increased care he required was beyond her physical ability. Now she lived alone in their large home on the lake, way back in the boonies. Her family all live in other locations, and visitors are few way out there. However, visiting hubby faithfully, church, lunching with friends, and her Red Hat activities seemed to keep her life full and satisfying enough.

That meeting day in October, Barb was so eager as we planned this November visit to our Red Hat Sisters at the CBRF, but—Barb never made it, except in spirit, in our spirits at least.

Less than one week following that October meeting, I received a painfully shocking phone call—Barb had died suddenly in her home! How could it be! Except for being frail in stature and the usual aging nuisances, she was relatively healthy. We had formed our group just two years before, open to all ladies within our church—(Grace Church—thus "The Red Hats of Grace"), and Barb was the first Sister we had lost. Later, as I read the newspaper obituary, I smiled; the list of her favorite activities finished with "she was a proud member of the Red Hats Group."

A number of us attended her Memorial Service, donned in Red Hats and full purple and red regalia. The bouquet we sent was in a red straw hat container, with a bright array of red and purple flowers. As some family members shared their memories, I was privileged to share on behalf of all her Red Hat Sisters. I hope I imparted not only our fond memories of Barb, but perhaps also our joy and love for one another and for the Lord…That is the desire of this Red Hat Group—as we embrace the overall philosophy of the original Creed we have adopted, written specifically for us as Christian Women, and as epitomized in Barb. It benefits our lives in general, when we honor Christ in all areas of our life…even as Red Hats Women!

With Barb's passing, I've had to accept the reality of impending loss in our ranks, considering the first rule of enrollment is being 60 years old or better…and the age of our group ranges from 65 to 90! I know now, by the Grace of God, we will face each loss with dignified sadness, and always with joy for having known them and shared this waning part of each life--Hoping that we have helped make it a little more pleasurable.

As I forced my thoughts back to this present gathering—I see even more of the *reality* of the golden years! Our host CBRF Red Hat Sisters sit around the tables, some eating their dessert with great delight, chatting gaily with us and each other; others need a little assistance eating and smile for joy with each mouthful. Looking around that room, listening to the laughter, noticing the diversity of appearance, actions, cognizance—my heart flooded with thankfulness to God for His grace and goodness in any stage of life…Once more, I'm reminded of the words of Jesus: "My *grace* is sufficient for you, for my power is made perfect in weakness." (2 Corinthians 12:9) And I think…"What a precious array—these *assorted shades of grace!*"! *"For we are God's workmanship, created in Christ Jesus…*(Ephesians 2:10)

Leaving wasn't easy amid much thanks and the pleas to, "Please come back" and "Please don't forget us." We assured them we won't forget; we're all Red Hat Sisters—in Christ!

Indeed, we'll all go back—even if some, like Barb, are there only in spirit! That could even be me—Only God knows!

The Lord will watch over your coming and going both now and forevermore.
—Psalm 121:8

Thanks for the Memories

(A Friend Turns Eighty)

What can I say, where should I start,
So many memories etched deep in my heart.
Memories sweet—in our old age to savor;
Memories that tell of God's ongoing favor.

Memories…

Husbands and families—fires kept burning;
Prayer groups, Bible studies—hearts always yearning.
We shared laughter and tears, as years swiftly passed by;
We now "stay the course" with our eye on the sky.

Of course there were times when it was hard not to doubt,
But by faith we were able to stand up and shout:
"Grace! Grace!"…To press on and endure,
And hold to His hand—ever strong, ever sure.

Memories…

What's it all about dear friend of mine?
This turning eighty?—I'm not far behind…
Practicing His presence? Hearing His voice?
In sunshine or storm, making His will our choice?

Only a moment since dawn—at life's starting line;
Now twilight sets in, but there's always *son*-shine;
We rejoice in the day, when truly we'll see,
Our Lord—Face to Face—for Eternity!

"I always thank God for you because of His grace given you in Christ Jesus. For in Him you have been enriched in every way...Therefore you do not lack any spiritual gift as you eagerly wait for our Lord Jesus Christ to return. He will keep you strong to the end, so that you will be blameless on the day of our Lord Jesus Christ. God, who has called you into fellowship with His Son Jesus Christ our Lord, is faithful."
—2 Corinthians 1:4-9

Heartfelt Thanks

(An Acrostical Thank You)

H eavenly places draw me near,
E ternity is mine.
A wesome God my heart doth revere,
R apture so divine;
T o know He bled and died for me,
F reeing my heart from sin.
E mmanuel – He lives in me,
L ikewise, I live in Him.
T *hanks be to God, all glorious!*

T here is no need He shan't supply,
H ope of the ages—ever;
A doring Father – His child am I.
N aught from His love can sever.
K nees bowed, with thankful heart proclaim:
S *avior...My Lord...forever!*

~~~~~~~

Grace Comes Before Thanks-giving

My heart overflows; each day is Thanks-giving
For all my world was once simply dross.
God's love and grace has made life worth living,
My thanksgiving began at the cross.
Oh, grace so sufficient, grace will exceed
All daily needs. From sin I'm set free.
My thanks I now offer, in both word and deed,
May others see daily, grace-thanks in me.

To Thanksgivings Past

The Child within me wants to sing,
When I remember little things...
Like "Thank you for the world so sweet,
Thank you for the food we eat,"
Childlike and simple, no need to impress,
Touching God's heart, with endearing caress.
"Thank you for the birds that sing...
Thank you God for everything."

~~~~~~~

<u>WINTER</u>

A Time of Rest,

Reparation,

And Growing in Grace

~~~~~~~

Suddenly it's Winter!

Lord, what happened to the autumn of my life? The *spring of my youth* was so long ago I can scarcely remember. Summer is just a passing fancy in my mind—but what happened to autumn? Wasn't I there just yesterday?

As we get older, time has a way of moving quickly and catching us unaware of the passing years. I look in the mirror and some elderly lady looks back at me! I suppose I should take comfort in the fact that this is the oldest I've ever been so far…but I'll never be this young again either!

Some things I remember well—such as when I was still young, just married and embarking on my new life. Yet in a way, it seems like eons ago, and I wonder where all the years went. I know that I lived them all—I have both scars and rewards as evidence…I still have glimpses of how it was back then—the good and the bad, the ups and the downs… All those hopes and dreams—many realized and many not. However, I am aware now, that most of those not realized were really not so important. And here I am in the winter of my life and it catches me by surprise! How did I get here so fast, so "all of a sudden?" Where did the years go? Where did my babies go? My youth? Spring and summer have slipped away; autumn too—and Suddenly It's Winter!

I can well remember through the years watching older people, never thinking, that season of my life would come so soon. But here it is… we are long retired and getting very gray, slow, wrinkled, and fragile. My true love—the man I married was virile, young and strong, full of energy; but like me, his age can no longer be denied; the change is there to see—and "energy" to him is one of those new drinks that young people buy—*we* are now those older folks we used to see – and never thought we'd be…Well, not quite so soon at least!

Each day now, I find that just getting a shower and shampoo is the real chore for the day—and taking a nap is no longer a voluntary luxury, it's mandatory—if I don't nap by choice—I ultimately just fall asleep wherever I sit!

Given no choice, I must face the reality of this new season of my life. I am determined, with your help, Lord, by Your strength, to cope with things such as all the aches and pains, the diminished strength, straining to do things I once took for granted. I have found that God is good—He hasn't changed, He is just as faithful to *supply all my needs according to His riches in glory* (Philippians 4:19) today as He was through all my yesterdays. Now that my winter has come, I can't be sure how long it will last, only God knows. But this much I do know: When it's over I will enjoy a new life of Eternal Spring at home with my Lord—and there await my loved ones, as they arrive —one by one when their seasons on this earth have come to an end.

Friend, are you aware that the summer of your life is waning? No matter what your age…perhaps it's only Spring, Summer or Autumn, but *Winter IS coming on*. God warns that our life is like a vapor that quickly vanishes away—so do what you can today—every day…Say and do the things you most want your loved ones to remember. Don't ever forget—you can never be sure when you may have to face a *spiritual* winter—no matter the date on your birth certificate. You will only make it through by holding tightly to His hand and believing His Word.

> Moment by moment I'm kept in His Love,
> Moment by moment I've life from above;
> Looking to Jesus till glory doth shine;
> Moment by moment, O Lord I am Thine.[15]

---

15 Daniel W. Whittle; May W. Moody—Public Domain.

Stand Still—Behold!

When storm clouds gather round me
And I strain to see the light;
When the enemy's advancing,
And I'm filled with doubt and fright,
I need only turn to Jesus,
My Savior tried and true,
Saying, Lord, I'm weak and weary
And I know not what to do.

Then, He speaks sweet peace to me...

"This battle, too, is mine, My child,
There's no need for you to fight.
Set yourself—I AM is with you,
Praise your God—Behold His might!
As you stand still—KNOW I AM GOD!
Have faith—take courage in my Word...
Sing, give thanks! My love endures,
Behold...the salvation of your Lord."

Based on 2 Chronicles 20

Be Still and Know

It was a beautiful crisp, winter evening as I stepped out on our deck to give the entry rug a quick shaking. I noticed I did not hear the sound of the wind chimes on the garage. I normally welcome the tinkling melody, like a gentle and soothing canticle, written on the wind by the hand of God. However, for days now we'd had extremely high winds almost constantly, day and night. The kind that kept the chimes ringing at a pitch more like clanging brass.

This evening, however, the silence got my attention. I quickly became aware of the perfect calm—so calm the chimes did not move. The crisp, cool air was invigorating and nothing was stirring. I sat there a moment, very still, just *listening* to the silence—you could have heard a pin drop in the soft new snow. It was so calming, so peaceful, I wanted to linger awhile. Perhaps this is what God meant for us to experience when He said, "Be still and know that I am God." (Psalm 41:10)...Linger, listen, hear my heart.

Part of me really did want to linger awhile longer, but the roast was in the oven, the cake needed frosting, the potatoes needed peeling. AND more importantly, (if the truth be known), it would soon be time for my daily TV ritual with Wheel of Fortune! No time for stillness and silence now! I think I might have heard God say, *"But if not now—when?"* With that, I busied myself in the kitchen where I could more easily ignore my thoughts (or was it His voice)?

Yes, it takes *time* and *discipline* to be still and listen. Hear what Author, Teacher and Pastor Chuck Swindoll says concerning Psalm 46:10: "Silence is the by-product of being still...When we commit ourselves to periods of absolute uninterrupted silence...we discover who God is—look at that verse: *Cease (Hebrew translation) so that you might know that I am God.* The Spirit of God reveals Himself when we shut out loud *or* busy distractions, when we close our mouths for a protracted period of time and *listen*…I do not believe anyone can become a deep person *(of God)* without stillness and silence."[16]

Ron Mehl, in his book <u>*What God Whispers In The Night,*</u>[17] relates watching a TV interview with Mother Theresa:

Several years ago, former CBS News Anchor Dan Rather found himself unprepared for this quiet, humble, but feisty little lady. Here is Ron's description of Dan's encounter with this humble and gracious nun:

"Somehow all his standard approaches and formula questions were inadequate for the task. And the little nun from Calcutta, sitting beside him so sweetly and tranquilly, didn't seem inclined to make his task easier.

"When you pray," asked Rather, "what do you say to God?" "I don't say anything," she replied. "I listen."

Rather tried another tack… "Well, okay…when God speaks to you then, what does He say?"

"He doesn't say anything. He listens." Rather looked bewildered. For an instant he didn't seem to know what to say…

"And if you don't understand that,' Mother Theresa added, "I can't explain it to you."

Don't you just love it! And her admonition is not only for Dan Rather, but us as well. We, too, have to search out the mystery and the *blessing* of this truth for ourselves. "…In quietness and trust is your strength…" (Isaiah 30:15)

In Proverbs 2:1-5 NLT, we find excellent directives for "searching and finding" the knowledge of God. *"For the Lord grants wisdom! From*

---

16   So You Want to be Like Christ? By Charles R. Swindoll; copyright 2005; W Publishing Group, div. of Thomas Nelson Inc.

17   By Ron Mehl; 2006; Multnomah Publisher's

His mouth come knowledge and understanding." If we are obedient to His directives, God will honor His Word and He will reveal Himself. We must never understate this promise, God does reveal who He is, and what He's about—through His Holy, inspired, anointed Word—The Bible. But, if we refuse to seek out times of silence and solitude with Him, we may gain knowledge *about* God without really *knowing* Him in the intimate way He desires. It is in these times of sustained stillness before Him that He often reveals Himself to us *intimately.*

But I have stilled and quieted myself, just as a small child is quiet with its mother. Yes, like a small child is my soul within me. (Psalm 131:2)

~~~~~~~

<u>Christmas</u>

Winters' Joy to the World

~~~~~~~

The Incarnation

The Christmas Season...A time when Christians around the world focus on one marvelous point in time. With concerts, children's plays, Christmas Carols, and joyous events of all kinds, we celebrate the birth of a Babe born in a manger—more than 2000 years ago.

Amid all the excitement, the anticipation, the hustle-bustle of preparation, let's pause a moment. Let's ask ourselves an important question... Beyond all the commercial hub-bub the world makes, *what does the miraculous birth of Jesus Christ into the human family have to do with us?* What does it mean to our families and others? Some who are living among the daily struggles of this troubled world?

My Friend, the way in which you embrace Christmas has everything to do with the way you spend this life—and the way you spend eternity!

> "The *virgin* will be with child and will give birth to a Son,
> and they will call him Immanuel,
> which means—God with us." (Matthew 1:23)
> <u>That</u> is **The Incarnation**

The Incarnation is a term meaning that the Second Person of the Trinity—*without ceasing to be God*—condescended to become a human being in order to save us from our sins, and to reconcile us to Himself—*The Incarnation* teaches us that God did not send someone else, such as an angel, to represent Him and do the appalling work of redemption, rather, He came Himself... *"The Word became flesh and made His dwelling among us."* (John 1:14)...The angel said to the virgin: *"You will be with child and give birth to a Son, and you are to give Him the name Jesus."* (Luke 1:31)

The Word—Jesus—Immanuel...God With Us

So, what does the Incarnation mean to you who are sad or lonely, perhaps mourning...in pain, physical angst... elderly or infirm...Or to those who are on the battlefields of the world—and their families? What special message does it bring? Simply put it means—God *IS* with us—He IS with you! And yet today, the words of Dr. A.W. Tozer still ring true: "He is still in the world, but mankind scoffs in its ignorance of Him, almost completely unaware of His revelation that the Word (Jesus Christ) can be known and honored and loved by the human heart."[18]

Does our faith in Christ assure us we will not experience hardship, pain, difficulty? Of course not! However, the Incarnation declares loud and clear: whatever we are going through—He has experienced it; He understands, and He will go through it with us.

> *"For I am the Lord, your God, who takes hold*
> *of your right hand..."* (Isaiah 41:13)

Jesus, *The Incarnation Himself,* spoke these words as He prepared to ascend back to heaven: "...surely I am with you always, even to the end of the age." (Matthew 28:20)

Jesus came to bring heaven to earth, to bestow the gift of sonship and bring you into a <u>personal *relationship*</u> with your Heavenly Father. His kingdom dwells within you.

Let's celebrate the reign of the King of Kings in our lives!

That is just *some* of what The Incarnation means to each of us, individually.

---

18   A Treasury of A.W. Tozer, chapter 37. (Grand Rapids; Baker, 1980)

Optional But Essential…

Observing Advent—the four Sundays before Christmas can be an exceptionally inspiring exercise of worship…Occurring in the same time frame is the busiest time of the year…that one month space between Black Friday and Christmas Day. Do we take the opportunity it offers us—to pause and wait serenely on God—Immanuel? That is actually what Advent is meant to be; a period to express our growing anticipation as we remember the coming of the Christ.

Historically, Advent has been a part of the church calendar since the fourth century. Most traditional Christian denominations have observed Advent to some degree since the onset. Others did not embrace it until the past generation or so; and some still do not. It is my personal opinion, derived from my own background, the reason they do not is a misunderstanding of the original intention. Some believed it to be an empty, superfluous *ritual*—more for show than for worship; which is not at all true when understood and approached as intended. It is meant to be a time of revisiting the drama as recorded in God's Word…Of reaffirming our faith and devotion to Him—in humility, surrender, love and worship…A time of *preparing our hearts* to be completely devoted to honoring Christ in *everything* as we plan and remember.

Advent is more than just an observance—it is a time of celebration—we celebrate what it means! It is traditionally observed in our homes and churches with a wreath holding four purple candles with a white candle in the middle. One purple candle is lit on each of the four Sundays leading up to Christmas Day, and the white "Jesus" candle is lit on either Christmas Eve or Christmas morning. The purple candles represent four of the persons and places prominent and essential to this Christmas Saga.

However, Advent is not meant to be just a symbolic lighting of candles… The first two Sundays represent a period of repentance as we recognize the darkness in and around us and our need of a Savior…the third

Sunday represents that rising hope in the promise that the Savior draws near. Then the fourth Sunday is bursting with anticipation—Jesus' birth is at hand!

Unfortunately, the Christmas season often becomes the most chaotic time of year. With just one month between Thanksgiving and Christmas Day, it seems there is little time for reflection. We are plunged into the craziness of *decorating, card sending, gift buying, wrapping, cooking, baking, etc.* All with the pressure of hurry, hurry, hurry! Our goal almost becomes one of simple survival rather than attention to the Lord, and celebrating His birth in thankfulness and worship. Consequently, very few of us are truly *ready* when the day arrives. Add to all the above preparation, the regular day-to-day activities and it's really hard to be ready—physically—but how much more important it is to be ready in worship and in spirit!

One of the Scripture readings often used in churches when lighting the Advent candles are the words of John the Baptist, "Prepare the way of the Lord."(Matthew 3:3) John came as a voice crying in the wilderness, calling on God's people to prepare for the Christ, their Messiah. Today the celebration of Advent can be our obedient answer to that call, "Prepare (make ready) the way of the Lord." But all too often we are ill-prepared. Why?

To prepare the way for the Lord sometimes requires clearing many other things out of the way. After all, our readiness is not measured by gifts, food, miles, postage stamps, successful parties, plays and concerts…But by responding to the call of God to quiet attentiveness to His presence… *In quietness and trust is your strength.* (Isaiah 30:15) *Be still and know that I am God.* (Psalm 46:10)…at least long enough to observe and celebrate Advent!

The Lord still cries out to us with the challenge to "prepare," to "make ready the way of the Lord." But, to wait on the Lord acceptably—we may have to change our pace, lose that sense of hurriedness and urgency to do "things."

...Let Jesus set the pace and determine
what is most important this year.

**"...*Your kingdom come, Your will be
done, On earth as it is in heaven.*"**
*(In other words—"Father God, I allow you to establish
Your kingdoms will priorities in my life today.)*
—Matthew 6:10-The Lord's Prayer

Are you ready?

Tell the Children

(Conversation with a child)

Please, Sir, tell me a story—a Christmas story;
Tell me a story to bring my heart cheer.
I want to hear a good Christmas story,
But not the one about Santa's reindeer.

A story that's happy, well, not too very sad;
Not Frosty the Snowman,
Or the one Charlie Brown had;
Please tell me a story, a new Christmas story...

Child, I'll tell you a story that never grows old,
First heralded by angels, to shepherds so bold.
A story of hope, sung with praises and joy,
Of the simple birth of a small baby boy.

Come, let me tell you the real Christmas story
Echoed down thru the years, to each age and race.
Yes, I'll tell the real story, **God's Christmas Story**...
Of **Jesus, a Savior,** *and love's saving grace.*

A Simple Advent Devotion

For Christmas Eve or Morn

(This is intended to be an "outline" so to speak—to be filled in with each candle as desired.)

Bible Reading: Matthew 1:18-24 followed by Luke 2:1-20, from a contemporary translation.

Let's review a few of the specific events surrounding the birth of Christ, as we light the Advent candles…Each candle represents a specific essential in the story of the birth of Christ.

(Light the first candle—the *prophecy* candle.)

When we light the prophecy candle, we are reminded…as recorded in the Bible hundreds of years earlier, that God spoke through the prophets of old many times, telling the people that they would have a Savior. Jesus means Savior.

For instance, the prophet Isaiah said—"Behold! The virgin shall conceive a child! She will give birth to a son, and will call Him Immanuel; which means God with us." (Isaiah 7:14)

And—"Unto us a child is born, unto us a son is given…and His name will be called Wonderful, Counselor, Mighty God, Everlasting Father, Prince of Peace." (Isaiah 9:6)

And the prophet Micah said—"Oh you, Bethlehem, are only a small village in Judah. Yet a ruler of Israel will come from you, one whose origins are from the distant past." (Micah 5:2-5 NLT)

And that brings us to the second candle—the *Bethlehem* candle.

(Light the candle.)

Micah went on to say—The people of Israel would be abandoned to their enemies until after He is born. They knew Jesus would be born in Bethlehem, God said so—but—Mary and Joseph lived in Nazareth of Galilee.

(Light the third candle, the *Shepherds'* candle.)

Read Luke 2:8-20...The shepherds played an important part in announcing the birth of Jesus—after they went and found the baby in Bethlehem, just as the angels had told them--they went to tell everyone...they helped spread the word.

The fourth candle is the Angel candle. (Light the candle.)

Think how much the Angels were involved as the messengers from God in the birth of Jesus... An angel appeared to Mary to tell her she had been chosen to be the virgin mother of the Messiah; then an angel appeared to Joseph to confirm to him that Mary was really pregnant by the Holy Spirit, and he should not abandon her. Then, the night He was born, the angels told the shepherds, they told them all about this special Christ Child, and the shepherds told everyone! And everyone was amazed! But the Bible tells us that Mary treasured all these things in her heart, and thought about it often.

It is Christmas Eve (or Morn)—now we will light the middle candle—the Jesus candle, and worship Christ our Savior and Redeemer—Immanuel, God with us.

Sing your favorite Carols honoring the birth of Christ as you sit in the glow of the candles—representing "Jesus, the light of the world."

The Joy of Belief

Lord, I believe, help my unbelief...

Recently I've noticed a new trend in Christmas Décor...Plaques, or-
naments, trinkets, various items—all declaring *"Believe...I Believe...
Be a Believer;"* etc. Even the famous Macy's Department Store has
used it in their advertisements, stating simply, BELIEVE!—MACY'S.
There is one I liked—a cute WELCOME sign for the door; it's a
Snowman Family saying, "A Family of Believers Lives Here." I can't
help thinking...believers? In what? Christmas? Jesus? Santa? Or
just—"WHATEVER?"

Remember <u>THE POLAR EXPRESS,</u> the children's book that Tom
Hanks turned into a very popular movie released at holiday time a
few years ago? It was a fantasy primarily for youngsters, but it did
provide some provocative spiritual truths for adults as well. The
main point comes with the climax of the story—the young lad
receives a gift from Santa—a bell that fell from his reindeer's harness!
When the *ringer* becomes lost, the boy finds that he can still hear
the bell ring even though others cannot, because *in his heart he truly
believes (*in Santa)!

And that is what happens if we truly believe...in Jesus Christ—His
Virgin birth, crucifixion, resurrection...He places a sort of "joy bell"
within us when we follow Him...As Jesus says in (John 15:11), *"I tell
you this, so my joy may be in you, and your joy may be complete."*

Satan tries again and again to cause our inner joy bell to *lose its ringer*—
we must continue to truly believe—in Jesus Christ the Son of God, and
all He wants to be *to us*...Savior, Prince of Peace, Counselor, Healer,
Baptizer, Coming King...*our All In All,* the source of our joy! If we
listen closely, *believing,* we can always have joy bells ringing in our heart!
In his epistle, Peter says of Jesus: *"Whom having not seen you love. Though*

now you do not see Him, yet believing you rejoice with joy inexpressible and full of glory." (1Peter 1:9) Even if Satan tries to steal our ringer, belief in Jesus will always keep joy bells ringing in our heart. Satan cannot rob us of that—only we can.

At times life throws us a curve in our personal lives and in our corporate lives. Such times as now...Our nation faces one of the worst financial crises of all times, and we can't seem to find the answers; the political climate has been more perplexing than usual; wars keep popping up all over the world. Many disturbing, yes, even threatening situations... what are we to do? We pray and believe God—(*believe: place confidence in, trust, rely on*)! God IS still in control—He DOES have a plan for us and for our nation. If we pray and believe, we will make it through. (In His time) God will win out! He has a plan of action and it's ultimately in our favor, Christian friend!

Are you struggling to believe? Remember the Father in Mark 9:14-29 who came to ask Jesus to heal his son. When Jesus said to him, "All things are possible to them who believe," he exclaimed: "Lord, I believe—help my unbelief!" *The boy was immediately healed.* If you're struggling with unbelief, do as that Father did...tell God—God will honor that—He WILL help you!

"The one grand plan God has for us is—ONLY BELIEVE! Absolute rest—Perfect submission. God has taken charge of the situation... because you DARE to ONLY BELIEVE what He says!" (Smith Wigglesworth)[19]

My Friends, keep the joy bells ringing, don't be embarrassed...As Christmas approaches, listen for the bells pealing out the promise of hope, faith and peace in Christ. Sing—joyfully, confidently...the following words of belief and hope. Words written so many years ago, by one of America's early renowned poets...Words that present some of the same despair as we face today—and yes, the same hope—in

---

19   Smith Wigglesworth (1859-1947), a British evangelist, who was important in the early history of Pentecostalism.

the same God and Savior, as the author held—one-hundred-fifty years ago...

I HEARD THE BELLS ON CHRISTMAS DAY...
Their old familiar carols play,
And wild and sweet, the words repeat
Of peace on earth, good will to men.

I thought how, as the day had come,
The belfries of all Christendom
Had rolled along the unbroken song
Of peace on earth, good will to men.

And in despair I bowed my head,
There is no peace on earth I said;
For hate is strong and mocks the song,
Of peace on earth good will to men.

Yet pealed the bells more loud and sweet,
God is not dead nor doth He sleep;
The wrong shall fail, the right prevail,
With peace on earth, good will to men.

Then ringing singing on its way,
The world revolved from night to day—
A voice, a chime, a chant sublime
Of peace on earth, good will to men.[20]

Longfellow first wrote this poem on <u>Christmas day in 1863</u>; it was first published in 1865 in a magazine. The music most widely used was added in 1872 by John Baptiste Calkin.

There are two additional stanzas not often heard. The words make reference to the pain and carnage of the Civil War, which prompted some of the "despair" Longfellow was feeling...As he listened to the

---

20   1863 by Henry Wadsworth Longfellow.

Christmas bells ringing out a message of "peace on earth, good will to men," the response was, "There is no peace on earth." He had lost his wife in a fire; his son had entered the war against his wishes, and was just recently severely wounded. But—the carol concludes with the renewed hope—"God is not dead, nor doth He sleep...the wrong shall fail, the right prevail"...

Daystar

O-o, Star of Wonder, Star of night,
Star with royal beauty bright,
Westward leading, still proceeding,
guide us to Thy perfect light.[21]

How I enjoy the lovely strains of familiar carols proclaiming the birth of our Savior as we joyously celebrate this most beautiful season. The above carol dates back to 1857, but is seldom heard in recent years. Occasionally perhaps, in Elementary and Sunday School Christmas plays—usually accompanying several very bored-looking fourth or fifth grade boys…All decked out in makeshift royal-like robes, paper crowns—and bearing gifts. The words, however, do lend themselves to a wonderfully inspiring truth from God's Word.

When the Magi from the East sought out the Christ Child, they knew if they kept their eyes fixed on that special star, it would lead them to Him—and the answers to many questions.

In their search, they had to cross the hot desert, ford rivers, climb steep hills, and face many hardships from the elements. But, they fixed their eyes on the Star—and so, reached the destination *God had set before them.*

Today, even at this happy time, many are experiencing serious trials of their faith, and wondering…*where will it all lead?* Where is that guiding light to lead them out of this time of despair? Have you ever wished God would do something like that for you? Place some sort of special guiding light in the heavens, so you could follow it on this journey of life? Well, in a sense He has…we find the promise in Psalms 32:8 NKJV…

---

21 We Three Kings; written in 1857, by Rev. John Henry Hopkins

"I will instruct you and teach you in the way you should go; *I will guide you with My eye*." WOW—think about that!

I wonder, are we sometimes just a little too earthbound? Do we often forget we are only sojourners here—that it's all so temporary? Help us, Lord, to remember we are on our way to a better place... a place prepared for us—forever to be with our Lord—the Christ!

Like the Wise-men of old, we will have to ford rivers, cross deserts and climb mountains; but we, too, have a great heavenly guide—*the eye of the Lord.* And He has promised to be with us through it all! *"When you pass through the waters, I will be with you; and when you pass through the rivers they will not sweep over you. When you walk through the fire you will not be burned; the flames will not set you ablaze."* (Isaiah 43:2)

The only way to follow is to keep our eyes on Him *and His guiding eye!* We don't need binoculars—God's unfailing Word will keep us focused as we *keep our eyes fixed on Jesus—the author and finisher of our faith..."* (Hebrews 12:2) The journey will be worth it all—the rewards so great—so eternal!

Thank you, Father, that you are always ready to lead us—help us to always be eager to follow. Lead us anew as we fix our eyes on Your guiding eye...Our—DAYSTAR,[22] Jesus...Star of wonder—Star of night, Star with royal beauty bright...

Lead On O King Eternal...Immanuel

---

22   2 Peter 1:19 KJV

I Wish You Joy...

...The Lord has come—to the world!

Would you agree that it would be a good thing if we gave more con-centrated thought to the individual words and phrases of the beautiful carols we sing at Christmas? Many of them have a profound year 'round message.

Every year as the Christmas Season arrives, the beloved carol "Joy to the World" rings throughout the land—over radio and TV, in schools, churches, stores, outdoor speakers, even in our heads—but how about our hearts and spirits? As the lyrics imply, this JOY *is* for the world; but it also states that each of us must receive it individually—personally..."*Let every heart prepare Him room...*" Just as John the Baptist cried: "Prepare the way of the Lord." ... to possess this joy we must make room for Jesus in our heart and in our life.

JOY to the world...is yours a joy that mostly comes at Christmas season and often exits (for the most part) on January 2? Or, is it the kind of joy King Jesus has in mind—everlasting joy? One apostle calls it—*inexpressible* joy! (1 Peter 1:8)

The Lord has come; but has He come—into your heart and life—per-meating your very being—every waking and sleeping moment? Paul tells us, "In Him we live and move and have our being." (Acts 17:28)... now that's quite a basis for inexpressible joy! Jesus desires that you experience *fullness* of joy—His joy. In John 15:11, He prayed, "That my joy may be in you, and your joy may be *complete*." That, my friend, means total, thorough, absolute! Living a life of overflowing joy does not depend on our circumstances, but it does depend on the Oneness with God such as Jesus enjoyed. His joy came from doing the will of the Father; even to the cross... "For *the joy set before Him He endured the cross*." (Hebrews 12:2)

By the by, let's not confuse joy with happiness…happiness is often *relative* to our circumstances; joy in Christ is *irrelevant* to our circumstances… "Count it all joy," James says. (James 1:2 NKJV) So, it's a matter of *simple arithmetic*—when you face trouble—your faith is being tested—that helps your endurance to fully develop—finally you are strong in character and ready for anything…*count it all* joy! (*Simple arithmetic.*)

Most of us have been blessed at times by someone who has a hearty, unrestrained laugh that seems to come from somewhere deep down inside, rising until it envelops their whole being, and erupts in torrents of contagious enjoyment, lifting spirits, and refreshing parched souls! Some old-timers would call it a "belly laugh."

I think, (maybe), that's what Jesus had in mind in The KJV of John 7:38, what do you think? *"He that believes in Me, as the scripture has said, out of his belly shall flow rivers of living water."* (He was speaking of the Holy Spirit.) In other words, an <u>outflow</u> of joy received <u>within</u> your being—then gushing forth to minister to others in the path of the flow… We've had a lesson in simple arithmetic—how about spelling… Can you spell J-O-Y?

Jesus and
Others and
You, What a wonderful way to spell joy;

Jesus and Others and You,
In the life of each Girl and each Boy,
J is for **Jesus,** for He has first place,
O is for **Others** we meet face to face;
Y is for **You** in whatever you do…Put yourself last and spell **JOY!**

Let's let the little boy and girl in us break out and minister…"become as little children…"

This Holiday Season and every day of every year, may *others we meet face to face*—see and know that *Joy has truly come to the world…if THE LORD*

HAS COME to your heart! Will our joy in Christ be the witness they need to see in order to believe it?

By faith—**Count it All Joy!**

~~~~~~~

Happy New Year!

~~~~~~~

My New Year Prayer for You

(Written by Paul the Apostle, used by permission)

"My response is to get down on my knees before the Father, this magnificent Father who parcels out all heaven and earth.
I ask Him to strengthen you by His Spirit—not a brute strength but a glorious inner strength—
that Christ will live in you as you open the door and let Him in.
And I ask Him that with both feet planted firmly on love, you'll be able to take in with all Christians the extravagant dimensions of Christ's love.
Reach out and experience the breadth! Take its length! Plumb to its depth! Rise to its heights!
Live full lives, full in the fullness of God.
God can do anything you know—
far more than you could ever imagine or guess or request in your wildest dreams!
He does it not by pushing us around but by working within us,
His Spirit deeply and gently within us."

—Ephesians 3:14-21 The Message Bible

I Pray You Enough

In Jesus name...

I pray you enough sun to keep your attitude bright no matter how gray the day may appear.

I pray you enough rain to appreciate the sun even more.

I pray you enough happiness to keep your spirit alive and everlasting.

I pray you enough pain so that even the smallest of joys in life may appear bigger.

I pray you enough gain to satisfy your wanting.

I pray you enough loss to appreciate all that you possess.

I pray you enough hellos to get you through the final good-bye.[23]

In Jesus name, Amen!

> Jehovah Jireh: God our Provider...El Shaddai:
> God our All Sufficient One
>
> He IS More than Enough!

---

23   author unknown

A New Year—An Open book

"You are an epistle of Christ…known and read by all men." —1 Corinthians 3:2

We're familiar with the saying, "His (her) life is an open book," sometimes used to describe persons of integrity/authenticity/transparency. Surely this is what Christ expects of all those who call Him Lord.

What an amazing gift a brand new year presents…A year's worth of opportunities, given to us by the Maker of heaven and earth, one sunrise at a time! Do you realize we are writing a diary of sorts? Not the kind with a clever little lock to secure from sight our secret thoughts, but an "open book," a "living epistle" for all the world to read.

We should view each day of this new year as a blank page, asking God to fill each one with some special inspiration. Most days will appear very ordinary, but God has a way of making them *extraordinary*. With Him as our guide, walking in His Presence, we can turn this virtual diary into an exciting handbook for victorious living!

Of course, each page will be sturdy stock, pure white—washed in the blood of Christ. (*"Cleanse me with hyssop, and I will be clean; wash me and I will be whiter than snow." Psalm 51:7)* The pages must be filled with love, understanding, truthfulness, integrity, helping your neighbor, giving to the needy…with the image of Jesus showing through on every page.

There should be chapters of testimonies about overcoming hardship—of fullness of joy in spite of trial; finding strength in Him when our resources have been used up…Of journeys, adventures, disappointments… Of gains and losses; laughter, and yes, tears. Each day's entry should depict a walk of faith…no words wasted focusing on what you *can't*, but focusing on what God *can*…Make it a tribute to the faithfulness of God's unfailing love and mercy…A truly open book, one you will be anxious to let everyone around you read—doing your best to give them a living picture of Christ...It IS what He expects of you...

He showed you, O man what is good...and what does the Lord require of you? To act justly, love mercy, and walk humbly with your God. —Micah 6:8

"Someone is watching you, wondering what
true Christianity is all about...
they may not believe your words, but they cannot deny your actions."
—Dr. David Jeremiah, in Turning Points Magazine

Waste Not—Want Not

Much is required from those to whom much has been given...Luke 12:48 NLT

"Only one life 'twill soon be past, only what's done for God will last."

Today is January 8, 2013—Elvis Presley's birthday; he would have been 78 years old. TV, Radio, Newspapers and internet are all sharing their ideas of Elvis memories. In the world of pop music, even 37 years after death, he is *"bigger than life."* Think about that phrase—how sad, how tragic. I still find my own emotional response much the same as on that fateful day, not for the same reasons that most mourn his death—but more because of the somber side of his wasted life.

Although I still qualified as young when Rock and Roll was "born" and Elvis was discovered, I never really embraced either; although I did enjoy his ballads and Gospel songs. And I related to Elvis in other ways...we were born on the same day, he one year later than I. We both grew up with a strong Christian background and a godly mother and grandmother, and worshipped in a good Pentecostal church. There he frequently raised that amazing, God-given, soul-stirring voice in glory and praise to God.

Yet, on August 16, 1977, pathetically, Elvis Aaron Presley slipped into eternity at age 42; his body bloated from years of abuse, medical mismanagement, prescription drugs, and all types of over indulgence—his life destroyed by the same diabolical forces as so many celebrities (and non-celebrities) before and since. Nearly two thousand years ago, the Apostle John warned against just such empty fallacies as those on which they all had based their lives: "the lust of the flesh and the pride of life." (1 John 2:16 KJV)

Ironically, the things Elvis left behind are of such insignificance for eternity...tarnished gold and platinum records, numerous autos, airplanes, etc...And Celebrity! All waste! Even though he adored his Mom, after her death he totally *wasted* the beloved memory of the love and devotion of a godly mother as well as that of God! His earthly mansion was called *Graceland*—but he neglected his heavenly citizenship and the *Mansion of Grace* prepared for him there. I can't say whether Elvis' heart was somehow prepared to meet the Lord on that fateful day in 1977, I prayed that it was. I do know—it's dangerous and foolish to gamble with our eternal soul for fame and baubles which will never satisfy—all the while gambling with our soul's eternal destination. *"What good is it for a man to gain the whole world, yet forfeit his soul? Or what can a man give in exchange for his soul?"* (Mark 8:36-37)

It should put us in mind of our own lives...What if we should have similar fame, fortune, notoriety, *even if it's on a smaller scale*—or what if we accumulate much goods, houses and expensive playthings—what difference does it make for eternity? Let's consider the words of one of the wisest, richest, most powerful, and highly respected men of all times, and once one of the most godly, King Solomon, who in his later years was greatly depressed...His innermost thoughts and feelings have been recorded in God's Word as a warning for us. Ecclesiastes 2: 4-11, 17-19. Read it *all* carefully. *"When I surveyed all that my hands had done, and what I had toiled to achieve, everything was meaningless; a chasing after the wind; nothing was gained under the sun."* Why was he so undone? I Kings 11: 4-6 will help us understand *"...as Solomon grew old...his heart was not fully devoted to the Lord his God."*

The lessons are clear—if we let God take a back seat in our drive for materialistic things, we too will become disillusioned—possibly drawn away from God. "Things" and "Celebrity" are so temporal, holding no lasting satisfaction—**no eternal value**. If we do gain them, we must always remember, and see that whatever we do—WE do it with ETERNITIES VALUES IN VIEW!

Jesus summarized the only *eternal* value system there is in Matthew 6:19-21; 33..."*Do not store up for yourselves treasures on earth, where moth and rust destroy...store up treasures in heaven...for where your treasure is—there*

your heart will be also. "Seek first the kingdom of God and His righteousness, and all these things will be added." And Jesus was speaking to a far
less materialistic culture than today—what would He say to us now?
Perhaps remind us...

> *"What good will it do a man if he gains the*
> *whole world, yet forfeits his soul—or what can*
> *a man give in exchange for his soul?"*
> —Matthew 16:26

> *The world asks, "What does a man own?" Christ asks,*
> *"How does he use it?"* (Andrew Murray)

"We can waste our lives on serving the devil and
end up in a flaming trash heap called hell,
Or we can spend our lives and resources on Jesus."[24]

---

24   Charisma on-line Daily devotional from Loving God, by Rod Parsley. 5/9/2013

Would-a; Should-a; Could-a…

Countdown to Next Year…

Here we are in a brand New Year; it seems last year passed me by so quickly. I'm sure some of you like myself, have taken a moment to survey some of the goals you had set for last year, and *woefully* sighed: "Would-a, should-a, could-a!" Then reluctantly put a few of them on your list for this year…

Soon February will be here—traditionally, the time by which most New Year's Resolutions have already been broken. If we seriously examine the "why" of this, I believe in many cases we will hear: "I would have—I should have—I could have—BUT…I just didn't have the time!"

I'm sure with most Christians this is not a lame excuse, but a cold, hard fact. We often have so little to say about how we use big chunks of our time…Your employer decides, obligations to the family decide, often the weather is a factor in making the decision; for some, physical limitations get the say. Nevertheless, we all have a certain number of hours for which we do have control…So, when we *do* get to make the decision of "who and what" is to take priority—how will we *choose* to spend those precious golden nuggets of time?

Time is a gift from God, so we are accountable to Him for how we use it. Does He take priority—beyond Sunday Church…mid-week church… Bible Study? All are important and good, as Paul admonished: *"Dear brothers and sisters be strong and steady, always enthusiastic about the Lord's work, for you know nothing you do for the Lord is ever useless."* (1 Corinthians 15:58 NLT) But, if Christ is our life, shouldn't He expect more?—More "devoted to Him alone" time? *"…I no longer live, but Christ lives in me…* (Galatians 2: 20)

What if we could watch the minutes of our life slipping away, like sands of time through an hourglass, what might we see—and think? Let's look at time through God's Hourglass...See how His Word directs us to use the time He has given us.

"Be very careful then how you live (redeeming the time), *not as unwise but wise, making the most of every opportunity, because the days are evil..."* (Ephesians 5:15-16) *"You are like a mist that appears for a little while and then vanishes."* (James 4:14) *(Lord), "Teach us to number our days aright, that we may gain a heart of wisdom; (Psalm 90:12) and again...*"Be wise—make the most of every opportunity.* (Colossians 4:5)

In other words, be carefully watching for God's "sacred appointments," lest we miss some. Let's ask God for *a heart of wisdom* in order to *number our days wisely* this year.

As I write, we still have before us 11 months...48 weeks...334 days...8016 hours...480,960 minutes! How will we spend them? Will we give *at least* the first 15 minutes of each day to God—**alone in His Presence?** How about the last 15 before we close our eyes in sleep? Not just a "Now I lay me down to sleep..." prayer-but *real time...* perhaps in the Word, with a good "devo" or good teaching book. Then as you lay your head on the pillow to go to sleep, make your last waking thoughts words of Thanksgiving, Praise and Adoration—the best sleeping remedy in the world! If you don't fall asleep as soon as you had hoped to—keep praising; what a wonderful time of communion you'll have with the Lord!

If we have surrendered our lives to Christ, every minute belongs to God...to seeing "His kingdom come, His will be done." Praying for His kingdom's will priorities to be established in our own life, must be a sincere moment by moment prayer; beginning the moment our feet touch the floor each day—or even before! And the last prayer at night before we fall asleep.

So, 15 minutes twice a day, morning and bedtime—*for God alone*; leaves me 470,940 minutes sandwiched in between...what kind of filling will you have in your "bread of life" sandwich? You can get an idea if you will "hear" the words of the beloved 14th Century Monk, Brother Lawrence, from the book, *The Practice of the Presence of God*...It was said of him that he could be found worshipping more in his kitchen than in his cathedral. He was often heard to say, "The time of business does not differ with me from the time of prayer, and in the noise and clatter of my kitchen, while several persons are at the same time calling for different things, I possess God in as great tranquility as if I were on my knees at the blessed sacrament. He said, "It is a great delusion to think that the times of prayer ought to differ from other times; we are as strictly obligated to adhere to God by prayer in the time of action, as by prayer in its season."[25]

Can we say that? Let's determine this year to spend <u>every minute in the presence of the Lord</u>—it *could* become a habit! He said, *"I am with you always..."* if He is with us always, shouldn't we be "with Him," really *"with Him"* always—ponder the alternative!

If all those numbers are just too many to get your brain around, try just "one day at a time"...24 hours—that's 1,440 minutes—minus 30 (and gaining) "alone in His presence." That's still 1,410 minutes left for me to follow in the path He leads, walking in the Spirit each step of the way. Then there won't be quite so many *sighs* of "woulda, shoulda, coulda," and more *proclaiming* of Philippians 3:12—*"Not that I already have obtained all this, or have already been made perfect, but I press on to take hold of that for which Christ Jesus took hold of me."*

The old year is gone, yesterday is gone—that's why they are "the past." Tomorrow is not here yet, and we can't borrow from it; it's the future we may never see. But today—Today is a gift—and that's why we call it the "present."

Lord, please help me always be more
present to Your *Presence*.

---

25   The Practice of the Presence of God; 1958, 1967 by Revell. Published by Spire Books, a div. of Baker Publishing Group

A Work in Progress

January, 1985

Contemplating the New Year ahead, I was prompted to go back in my journals about 10 years to search out what I had set as goals for that year—resolutions so-to-speak. I found an introspective collection ranging from practical, to physical, and, of course, spiritual. Such idealistic desires as—exercising regularly; losing 25 pounds; reading the Bible through; doing my hair differently, perhaps including a color change (it had looked the same way for at least ten years)…enrolling in a writing course at Nicolet Community College; and memorizing a new scripture verse each week.

Well, in retrospect, it seems it took me about three years to read the Bible through; I did lose the 25 pounds…however, during the ensuing years I have found it all again!

I never kept track of the total number of verses I memorized, it surely fell short of one per week…The hairstyle? Well, it did change somewhere along the way—and so did the color—naturally—from very dark-brown to a *natural* "salt and pepper"!

As for the writing course, it's on my list each year; I even began one once…that resolution probably should be replaced with a one pertaining to discipline and procrastination. It seems I decided to go the "self-taught" route.

Through the years I have often expressed much the same goals. It would be nice if I had accomplished more of them, and it is still my intention—some of them at least. However, 10 years of just living has put these goals and others I've had along the way into perspective. I find myself more concerned with improving on the inside, realizing the outside will always *reflect* what's on the inside. I'd like to improve in ways that are difficult to weigh or measure, except by God and His Word, lest I be "weighed in the balances and fail the test." (Daniel 5:27 NLT)

I long for a consistent spiritual exercise program, not available at the "Y"...One that will condition and develop "muscles" never really visible on the outside...Like being more sensitive to those around me, and responding accordingly, but quietly...taking more time to put my own desires aside to help others...To think before speaking, and then speaking only words of support and affirmation, realizing, sometimes the wisest words are those *unspoken*...To be slow to give advice, but quick to encourage...To be patient, loving, forgiving. Being less concerned with "accomplishing" and more with "becoming"...becoming the fragrance of Christ.

I am no longer determined to be "my own woman," but becoming "God's woman." I am no longer driven to "perform and impress," but more to "minister."

So, though I may not have been as successful as I'd like in fulfilling <u>my</u> goals, God has been at work in me all these years, by His grace—helping me to fulfill <u>His goals</u>...Breaking down my stubborn self, shaping and molding me, smoothing rough edges, and deepening my desire to be "more like Jesus." He still has a lot of work to do, but "I am confident that He who has begun a good work in me, will carry it on to completion until the day of Jesus Christ." (Philippians 1:6)

(Afterword): How cyclical life is—when the above piece was written, I was looking back 10 years. Now as I enter it into the manuscript of this book, another 28 years have passed...Much of it could have been written yesterday—with the same sincerity. Most of what I was concerned with then I must still keep before God daily, I'm still in the process of completion! Philippians 1:6 is my ultimate hope! Nevertheless, I am convinced that God looks favorably on our sincere efforts, recognizing—we are all an example of His "work in progress.")

Today Is the Day...

Today is the tomorrow you
worried about yesterday.

It's February 1ˢᵗ—have you broken your New Year's resolution yet? I personally gave up making resolutions for the New Year long ago. However, it does seem a suitable time to make changes—but then *every day* is a good day to determine to change for the better— add something new, discard some of the old, and strive for more consistency and less procrastination.

**It's never too late to start...Today is the
first day of the rest of your life.**

Most of us frequently determine to improve in areas such as—exercising, losing weight, eating healthy, hospitality, completing a project, being good stewards, helping others, etc.—and, oh yes, of course... More Bible study and prayer—DAILY! Therein, my friends, lay one of the secrets of successful change—*consistent* Bible study with prayer...

I can't guarantee you will lose weight, gain muscle, riches or fame—nor that you will become a King David, Sister Theresa or Dolly Madison★. I can guarantee by standing on the promises in God's Word, you will see some necessary changes in the "inner man/woman," change that will radiate outwardly, as God grows you in areas in which He knows you need to be changed and strengthened.

Reading the Bible through is a fine commitment, but we do need a *Scripture study schedule*, and it can be only a verse or so a day. If you miss a day or so, you needn't *necessarily* try to catch-up, if the stress of trying to catch up, makes you want to give up—just *get back on track and keep going*. And ask God to restore your zeal. Another good practice—take notes of scriptures used by the Pastors as they share—and take time to do a search on them during the week…Like the Christians at Berea, who after listening to Paul and Silas preach, *"searched the scriptures daily to find out if these things were true."* (Acts 17:11) We need to look for truth "as for hidden treasure" (Proverbs 2:4-5) Not just snacking, but feasting! *"Your Words were found and I ate them, they are my joy and my hearts delight."* (Jeremiah 20:16)

All this combined with prayer and worship can be truly life-changing when we make it a daily habit—with the sincere desire to know Christ better, love Him more deeply, and become more like Him. (Read Philippians 3:10) We can expect wonderful results such as—our vision becoming clearer, our gait livelier, our faith *(muscle)* stronger, our spiritual appetite satiated…our love deepened, our service broadened, our perspective heightened, our countenance brightened…and our territory enlarged!

Today is the day the Lord has made;
let us rejoice and be glad in it.

★(For you youngsters; Dolly Madison was First Lady to the fourth President—and became known as "the hostess with the "most-est"", helping to define the role of First Ladies for the future).

Alone in His Presence

Intimacy with God takes time, and there is no substitute for waiting in His presence, totally abandoned to Him.

God alone, my hiding place,
God alone, such sweet embrace,
God alone, all else denied,
God alone be glorified.

I in Him and He in me,
This my desire fore'er shall be;
Trusting always in His Word,
His constant Presence my reward.

One day I'll see Him face to face,
The One who saved me by His grace.
As I am known I then will know,
For God alone has deigned it so.

In **Revelation 3:17**, I believe Jesus is telling us…He has a special blessing for those who *extravagantly waste themselves in His Presence*—in private… Not just with pleas and petitions, but in adoring worship—basking in His Presence…sensing His shekinah glory. To those He will give to eat a special bread—a divine manna—Heaven's "hidden manna." And when they meet Him face to face, He will give them a white stone

---

26 The Glory of His Presence—1935, by Homer A. Rodeheaver

with a new name written on it—His own special name for them...A *nickname*...a term of endearment. A name no one else knows about. Even now, I believe if we listen closely in the Spirit, we can *feel* Him call us by that name—of course we don't *specifically* yet *know it*—but we sense it—in those special times as we sit at His feet, and enjoy the privilege of abiding long and often—<u>Alone in His Presence.</u>

"My presence will go with you and I will give you rest."
—Exodus 33:14

~~~~~~~

Valentine's Day

An Affair of the Heart

~~~~~~~

Love is always bestowed as a gift—

Freely, willingly, and without expectation...

We don't love to be loved;

We love to love.

Leo Buscaglia (Dr. Love)

Magnified Through Love

O Lord, our Lord,
how majestic is Your name in all the earth!
—Psalm 8:9

No one is like You, O Lord:
You are great, and Your name is mighty in power.
—Jeremiah 10:6

Oh, magnify the Lord with me,
and let us exalt His name together.
—Psalm 34:3

How majestic is Your Name...Yahweh,
You, O, God are as beautiful as Your Name...
Jehovah, Father, Almighty God, King of the Universe,
King of Kings, Lord of Lords, Great I Am,
Immanuel, Christ, Soon Coming King,
Alpha and Omega, Savior, Redeemer, Daystar.

What wondrous grace, so rich, divine
That links that lovely name with mine!

This God of heaven and earth loves me,
My heart cries out how can it be?
That He should love one such as me;
Can one so unworthy, love in kind—?
Live loved; love as He loves?
My heart o'erflows
And I, too, must so love...

For I am deeply loved, and fully forgiven,
Unconditionally, freely and bound for heaven.

My heart remembers...God IS Love!
And everyone who loves,
Lives in God—and God in Him!
Yes, as God so loved the world,
In Him my love is made complete,
In Him, I, too, can so love...

Oh love of God, so deep and pure!
Purify my love, may it ere endure.

All glory to Him, who alone is God our Savior, through Jesus
Christ our Lord. Yes, glory, majesty, power, and authority
belong to Him, in the beginning, now and forevermore.
—Jude 25

Unfathomed—Unending Love

The Holy Spirit knows me far better than I know myself,
Knows my weighty condition and keeps me before God.
That's why I can be so sure that every detail in my life of
love for God is worked into something good.

God knew what He was doing from the very beginning.
He decided from the outset
To shape the lives of those who love Him
Along the same lines as the life of His Son.

So, what do you think?
With God on our side like this, how can we lose?
Do you think anyone is going to drive a wedge
Between us and Christ's love for us?
There is no way!

Not trouble, not hard times,
Not hatred, nor hunger, nor homelessness,
Not bullying threats, not backstabbing,
Not even the worst sins listed in Scripture.

None of this fazes us because Jesus loves us.
I'm absolutely convinced that nothing...
Nothing living or dead, angelic or demonic,
Today or tomorrow, high or low,

Thinkable or unthinkable—absolutely *nothing*
Can get between us and God's love
Because of the way Jesus our Master
has embraced us.

—Romans 8:28-39 MSG

Virginia Phillips Kreft

> *Dear Friends, since God loved us that much,*
> *we surely ought to love each other.*
> *…let us stop just saying we love each other;*
> *let us really show it by our actions.*
> —1 John 4:11; 3:18 NLT

Do I Love Jesus?

Indeed I Do!

Why do I love Jesus?

I love Him because He first loved me" (1 John 4:19). I love Him because "He gave Himself for me (Titus 2:14). And of course, I love Him because "I have life through His death and peace through His blood." (Ephesians 2:13-15).

I love Him because "He is altogether lovely" (Song of Songs 5:16).

Friend, is there any question in your mind that you love Jesus— intimately, unconditionally—and that you have no doubt that He loves you as Paul has expressed in Romans eight? You *must* be sure—so sure you would stake your life on it! Are you able to say like Paul "I know who I have believed and am convinced that He is able to guard what I have entrusted to Him (2 Timothy 1:12). Don't settle for anything less than loving Him with a love that is so certain, that sharing that relationship is a constant reality—one that totally compels you to want to love Him more.

When we are sure of the extraordinary love He has for us, and we for Him, we are filled with a deep sense of His beauty—His holiness, His power. We will be filled with awe at His greatness, goodness and infinite perfection...our soul will be overjoyed, yet humbled in His presence... And in that presence is where we will always want to be...And we will continually have a song. Oh what wondrous grace that allows one such as I, to know such love as we share, Oh, Lord, my God and my Savior!

> "Jesus is the sweetest name I know,
> and He's just the same as His lovely name.
> And that's the reason why I love Him so...
> Oh, Jesus is the sweetest name I know."
>
> —Lela Long, 1924

A Friend Loves at All Times

—Proverbs 17:17

February presents us with three major observances: Presidents' Day (one day—two Presidents) and Valentine's Day...That one special day of the year designated to declare our love and affection—with some heartwarming gesture...to our spouse, family, parents and often special friends...Many are remembered with cards and even gifts of affection... But do we endeavor to live up to those glowing declarations the other 364 days of the year?

Have you ever wondered, what makes you or me a *special* friend? What are some of the more important qualities? What do your friends see in you that brings out the best in them? What do your friends *say* about you—*especially to others*?

They probably don't focus much on your looks or your charm—your attire or the car you drive. They are more likely to speak of far different virtues, such as...Your helping hands and how willing they are to come to the aid of others—your feet that go where there is a need. Often they will speak of your voice as—calming and encouraging, comforting, inspiring and your words affirming. Would they mention that you are willing to become involved in their lives, *right where they are*...like Jesus did? Perhaps you try to ease their conflicts with words of Godly wisdom and prayer?

Do you eagerly seek to maintain a deep connection? Friendship is an invisible, but very strong link binding you to those you care about. When you wrap yourself around the heart of a friend with the gentle embrace of God's love—it is one of the strongest of bonds: *"By yourself, you're unprotected. With a friend you can face the worst. Can you round up a third? A three stranded rope isn't easily broken."* (Ecclesiastes 4:12 MSG)

Our world is bursting with shallow devotion and feigned loyalty—but the friendship we are speaking of here is unique and rare. We are fortunate and greatly blessed if we experience only a few such friendships in our life...but how much more fortunate and blessed *to be* such a friend.

Go ahead, enjoy the flowers—the Chocolates and the Bon-Bons, even the Candy Kisses—they will truly gratify the taste buds for a moment, but one of the *greatest sweeteners* of human life is true friendship...it can last forever!

> God pairs people as friends at the right time,
> place and *season* of need.
> --Wayne Watson

> *Who could refrain that had a heart to love,*
> *And courage to make that love known?*
> William Shakespeare

Attitude Creates Reality

Your attitude reflects your view of God—Do you need an attitude adjustment? Heart Attitude that is…

"I am convinced that life is ten percent what happens to me and ninety percent how I react to it…and so it is with you; we are in charge of our attitudes."
—Charles Swindoll, Bible teacher and author

Let's pay a visit to…
The Great Physician's Heart Clinic
Located at the corner of Matthew 5:3-12 and Grace Avenue…
No appointment needed—No waiting—No fees!

Check out the rewarding *reality* of each *heart attitude adjustment*, and discover the *"sacred delight*[27] experienced with this heart procedure…it *will* require an *open heart*…

Consider Jesus' opening words in <u>The Sermon on the Mount,</u> that portion known as <u>The Beatitudes</u>—or "be"-attitudes. Unfortunately, many think of them as mere "Platitudes." That isn't what Jesus intended…He wanted to instill deep spiritual values, *defining the heart attitudes we must have to please God.* No doubt Paul had this teaching of Jesus in mind as he exhorted the church at Thessalonica, *"Dear brothers and sisters, we urge you in the name of the Lord Jesus to live in a way that pleases God, as we have taught you. You are doing this already, and we urge you to do it more and more."* (1Thessalonians 4:1 NLT) To do this, we may need an occasional adjustment…attitude adjustment…*heart* attitude that is!

---

27 Phrase used for the beatitudes by author Max Lucado in The Applause of Heaven.

*Attitude creates reality—so how you view a situation
can have an enormous impact on how you live.*[28]

That statement is a medical observation from the Mayo Clinic; it goes on, "researchers have clearly documented that having a more positive optimistic view of whatever you are faced with provides health benefits for many individuals."[29] This is so true of our life in Christ also; how can it not be since in reality "our life IS in Christ! *"In Him we live and move and have our being."* (Acts 17:28) Let's look at Jesus' prescription for a strong and healthy heart attitude…

A dependent attitude: *Blessed are the poor in spirit*…poverty of spirit is being spiritually needy and acknowledging we can do NOTHING without God's help. (Philippians 4:13) Don't be like the "rich young ruler" (Matthew 19:16-22)…it wasn't his money that hindered him from following Christ as much as his *self-sufficiency*…a very dangerous heart attitude in a Christian's life.

A repentant attitude: *Blessed are they that mourn*…How apropos that this attitude follows *poverty of spirit*…Jesus is referring here to "mourning", *as being sorry for our sins*—If we truly *mourn* over the sickness of our sins, repentance is the only antidote…God is not looking for perfect people, but obedient people, and He is deeply pleased, and we are deeply blessed if we make *genuine* heart repentance a daily habit.

A humble attitude: *Blessed are the meek*…Jesus, our great example, calls us to a meek and lowly heart attitude. He tells us that the secret to true strength and real leadership is a servant's heart. God's power is not as dependent on our *ability,* as it is on our *availability.*

An insatiable attitude: *Blessed are they that hunger and thirst for righteousness*…Jesus desires that we be passionate for more of Him. We

---

28 Mayo Clinic on-line Newsletter: mayoclinic.com/health/ mood-and-attitude—3/12/2013

29 Mayo Clinic on-line Newsletter: mayoclinic.com/health/ mood-and-attitude—3/12/2013

cannot settle for yesterday's manna, it becomes sour. If we allow the Holy Spirit to fill us continually, we will fast, pray, worship and pursue God with ever increasing fervor.

<u>A forgiving attitude</u>: **Blessed are the merciful**…those who are merciful are *shown* mercy—they witness grace. The most important trait of the merciful person is being quick to *sincerely forgive*. Forgiving others allows us to see how God has forgiven us. Jesus said *His love flows through the channel of forgiveness*; and we <u>cannot</u> know Him intimately if we refuse to forgive others.

<u>A transparent attitude</u>: **Blessed are the pure in heart**…A pure heart is a transparent heart…What are you hiding in your heart that you don't want others to see? Perhaps *you don't even want to see it*—Remember, God sees it…And if we don't admit it, repent and be free, it will do great damage to our heart. <u>The only thing necessary to hide in our heart is His Word</u>. (Psalm 119:11) Notice—all these *Spirit adjusted be-attitudes* are in perfect sequence: *recognizing our sin; repenting; being humble servants of God*…By now we're so filled with sacred delight we hunger and thirst *for more*! The more we receive, the more we *give,* and *forgive*…and that's *mercy!* And on it goes…*Pure—righteous*…heart-adjusted attitudes!

"The Christian faith is ultimately not only a matter of doctrine or understanding or of intellect, it is <u>condition of the heart.</u>"
—D. Martyn Lloyd-Jones)[30]

"When Jesus spoke of the heart, he spoke of the totality of the inner person—desires, perceptions, thoughts, intentions, will, faith, hope, love'[31]… *"Above all else, guard your heart, for it is the well-spring of life."* (Proverbs 4:23)

I'd like to challenge you to let the Holy Spirit once again "examine your heart"…Perhaps you need to undergo some delicate heart surgery…so

---

30   Studies in the Sermon on the Mount—D. Martyn Lloyd-Jones

31   Mayo   Clinic   on-line   Newsletter: mayoclinic.com/health/ mood-and-attitude—3/12/2013

you can live and walk in new freedom and experience this sacred de-light[32] overflowing in every area of your life…A heart that beats strongly in obedience to Christ's words will not suffer from <u>heart failure!</u>

"Biblical love is not emotions or feelings, but <u>attitudes</u> and <u>actions</u> that seek the best interest of the other person."[33]

FYI: Quotes in the Mayo Clinic newsletter[34] are based on a book, *The Road Less Travelled,* written by M. Scott Peck, noted American author and Psychiatrist (and a Christian), first <u>published in 1978 by Simon and Schuster</u>. It is, in short, a description of the attributes that make for a fulfilled human being, based largely on his experiences as a psychiatrist and a person. In my opinion, Although it is not considered a "religious writing" but more of a "medical observation," It seems to clearly point (especially in the final section) to "grace," and "miracles." When years earlier, as a little known psychiatrist, he first tried to get another well-known publisher to publish this work, it is reported they turned him down, saying the final section was too *"Christ-y."*

I believe it is noteworthy here, only because the medical world is using it to support their findings—that "attitude" plays a very huge part in our over-all handling of life in general—Jesus pointed this out over 2,000 years ago in the <u>Sermon on the Mount</u>—as recorded in the gospels! If we depend on the Word for all our life situations—we already know this…

"Attitude creates reality—
<u>*…How you view a situation can have an enormous impact on how you live!"*</u>

Come to think of it—**the whole Sermon on the Mount, is <u>ALL</u> about ATTITUDE!**[35]

---

32   Phrase used for the beatitudes by Max Lucado in The Applause of Heaven.

33   Studies in the Sermon on the Mount—D. Martyn Lloyd Jones

34   Mayo Clinic on-line Newsletter: mayoclinic.com/health/mood-and-attitude—3/12/2013

35   The Practice of Godliness by Jerry Bridges—NavPress Publishing, 1983, 1986, 2008

~~~~~~~~

A GOOD WORD

FOR

ANY SEASON!

~~~~~~~~

Always Begin With Praise

"Praise be to you, O, Lord,
God of our Father Israel,
from everlasting to everlasting.

Yours, O, Lord, is the greatness and the power
And the glory and the majesty and the splendor,
For everything in heaven and earth is yours.

Yours, O Lord, is the kingdom;
You are exalted as head over all,
Wealth and honor come from you;
You are the ruler of all things.

In your hands are strength and power
To exalt and give strength to all.
Now our God, we give you thanks,
And praise your glorious name.

—1 Chronicles 29:10-13 NLT.

The God of Abraham, Isaac and Jacob

In the name of Jesus, through faith in His name,
There is power to make us whole,
Glorified by the Father, seated at His right hand
He's perfecting us, mind, body and soul.

In the name of Jesus, through faith in his name,
God the Father will honor his Word.
For the God of Abraham His promise will keep
Did you not know—had you not heard?

In the name of Jesus, through faith in His name,
God the Father great wonders will do,
For the God of Isaac, the miracle child
Has a miracle just waiting for you.

In the name of Jesus, through faith in His name,
God the Father will change us today,
For the God of Jacob, a new man did create,
He's ever changing us now as we pray.

In the name of Jesus, through faith in His name
We see wonders of mercy and grace,
For the God of Abraham, Isaac and Jacob
Sent His Son to die in our place.

In the name of Jesus, through faith in His Name,
We'll victoriously keep running the race,
Till the God of Abraham, Isaac and Jacob
We will meet one day face to face.

Who Can Explain It?

"God is able to make ALL grace abound to you..."
—2 Corinthians 9:8

Who can explain it—the grace of our God?
That unmerited love and favor.
O, that I might fully define
That all-encompassing gift called grace.

My debt of sin is paid in full,
Freely I receive,
Walking daily in new mercies,
So great is His faithfulness.

Amazing grace—redeeming grace,
Matchless grace—marvelous grace,
Limitless, fathomless, abounding grace;
Grace sufficient for all my sin.

A hundred ardent adjectives will not suffice.

If I were to speak with a thousand tongues
The words could not define,
Should I commune in the idiom of angels
I would yet be at loss...

For angels know naught of redeeming grace.
And yet I know such grace...
By faith in God, through Christ,
This grace to me is bestowed.

Virginia Phillips Kreft

Day by day—hour by hour,
Moment by moment,
According to my need
His grace is sufficiently increased.

Even in the valley of despair, or on the precipice of death,
I need not fear;
For with whispering hope I will shout,
Grace! Grace! God's grace!

Who Can Explain It?

One Night in May

My heart o'erflows with love and pride,
My world feels starry bright,
As I hold God's precious miracle
In the quiet of the night.

He snuggles close upon my breast,
Our breathing seems as one,
As with his mother years before,
My beloved child firstborn.

Her firstborn now lies in my arms,
Blest continuity,
Of generations gone before
And those still yet to be.

As he sleeps—loved and secure
I caress his tiny hand,
With tears of joy and wonderment
Only Mothers understand.

My Daughter—My Friend

From the moment of birth you were
My daughter—my darling baby girl;
And soon that adorable toddler,
Who could set my heart awhirl.
Through childhood, teen years and beyond
I sensed a pleasing trend,
This baby, this child—too soon an adult,
Had become a special friend.

So many titles for the relationship phases
We've formed throughout the years,
Each one with its own special mixture
Of life's usual smiles and tears.
But my lovely, I can hardly believe
The phase we now begin…
The joy of growing old together,
You're a Senior Citizen !

Happy 55th Birthday Daughter

A Prayer for a June Bride

There she stands Lord, in her gown of pure white,
With Jeff by her side, her bright shining Knight.
Our precious child of twenty-one years
Of caring and sharing, of laughter and tears.
Time passes so quickly, seems just yesterday,
When we first stood before you to give her away...
To You Lord, with our promise to love and to nurture,
Dedicating to You her life and her future;
How often we've failed and found that we must
Commit her again, and again—to Your trust.

They stand here together, before God, family and friends,
Soon no longer two, here their singleness ends;
Her Father has just now spoken the word...
That we *give her away*—so all have heard.
We commit her to Jeff—and both to You,
Help us Dear Lord, to that vow to stay true.
With joy we receive him as our own dear son.
This moment as You unite them as one,
Our fervent prayer is—for all of their days
You remain Lord and Master, in all things—all ways.

~~~~~~~

...Further Lord, we thank you today
For two others who also are giving away,
Their own dear son, to our daughter to cleave,
They give him with love, and her they receive
Into their hearts, forever to stay;
Thank you Lord, and bless them we pray.

June 23, 1984

Two Roses

Two rosebuds placed within a vase
So lovely to behold,
And with some tender loving care
Their beauty will unfold.

They stand together in the vase
United at the stem,
Confident that loving hands
Will always care for them.

Tho they will wilt and dry with time,
With pluck, together now they stand,
For the Master Gardener cares for them
With a strong but gentle hand.

One day the petals began to recede,
To some their appeal has faded;
Still they stand, by us admired,
Their beauty never jaded.

Two people joined in marriage are
Much like these roses two,
Depending on the hand of God
To nourish them all life through.

As time goes by their union holds,
Though their strength begins to fade;
With graying heads they smile and say,
"We're still all the good Lord made."

And now they seem a little strained,
Their stems no longer agile,
To we younger folk so often hurried,
They smile and say, "Just sit awhile."

Like roses—so all marriages
Come with bloom and thorn,
They must be cared for gently
And not asunder torn.

These who celebrate today
Have persisted forty years,
God's loving hand has carried them
Through laughter and through tears.

We all now come together
On this cold December day,
To wish them well, and many more
As Jesus leads the way.

*Written by Chrystina (Kreft) Melau, in honor of her parents
fortieth Wedding Anniversary; December 5, 1993.
Used by permission.*

May Becomes December

Our day of spring had passed
It was summer at last,
We were young, and there we would stay.

We picnicked and ran,
Built castles of sand,
Watched waves come and wash them away.

We laughed and we played,
We cried and we prayed,
Life so full, so happy and gay.

Autumns passing now too,
And winter's in view,
As we look to God for each day—

Some nights feel so cold,
And we're getting old,
It's December—what happened to May?

My Husband

Today was one of those days Lord …I was doing quite well, until I became ill with this pesky virus that sent me to my bed. There is not much to be done about it but let it run its course—but how I longed for a little tender-loving care. Yes, my girls were in and out to bring what comfort they could—but it's not the same, Lord. Oh, how aware I am that my husband is no longer with me…How I miss him creeping in quietly—asking, "Do you need anything? His rough hand gently stroking my forehead, "Are you sure you don't have a fever?" Then just sitting there for a moment—patting me softly, as one would a child…Whispering, "You get some sleep now; you'll feel better in the morning…I won't go anywhere, I'll be right here."

Such memories bring tears as usual, but then I recall something you said, Lord, *"Your Maker is your husband—the Lord Almighty is His name!"*[36]

Yes Lord, I do feel Your gentle touch, Your hand on my aching brow— Your loving words whispering peace and assurance; letting me know you are right here—"I will never leave you or forsake you," You said. Thank you Lord, I'll sleep now; I'll see You in the morning—and yes, I'll feel better.

---

36   Isaiah 54:5

A Sacred Commentary

Reading our Bible should be like a conversation with a best friend we've come to visit with—picking up where we left off last time, never missing a syllable—as though we'd never parted...We recall past visits, good times—advice shared, counsel given, lessons learned—Much of it to sacred and treasured to be shared with any other—until after we share it with this special one...And so it is with God and His Word, we are always as close as what's "hidden in our heart."

Many of us have a favorite Bible Commentary or Bible Handbook to aid us into gaining a deeper comprehension of the Word of God. Not being learned authorities ourselves, we trust the insight and understanding of those who, under the anointing of the Holy Spirit make that their life's work. However, that same Holy Spirit will help to enlighten us as well—if we apply ourselves to reading and studying the Word prayerfully, with a desire for more insight.

One of the ways to reap the most from the Holy Spirit's enlightenment is to keep a "log" or "journal." How often I just happen to be reading a passage in the Bible and suddenly find the answer to a troubling situation I am facing. Or even reading a simple, familiar passage that suddenly has a profound impact on me as if I had read it for the first time...The Holy Spirit *enlightened* that scripture to reveal God's will... when that happens—<u>underscore it</u>...Write it down, bookmark it. Do this with every special promise or insight God gives you, soak up His Word...every verse that touches your heart...Remember, that is God's *specific Word for you*...Whatever challenge, or need you are facing—grab hold of that Word! Read it, meditate on it and <u>declare</u> it! When the enemy rises up with his weapon of doubt—stand your ground! God will raise up His standard against him—*drive him away by the breath of His Spirit...(*see Isaiah 59:19).

The revelation of God's heart, His will and purpose, becomes our heart, will and purpose...as we commune with Him through prayer and His Holy Word...a treasured record of our visits with Him.

"...as the Spirit of the Lord works within us, we become more and more like Him and reflect His glory more and more." (2 Corinthians 3:18 NLT)

Yes, you can build, grow and strengthen your life in Christ with your own personal *Bible Commentary*, receiving insight revealed by the Author Himself—your own "Sacred Commentary."

> *"listen to me and treasure my instructions. Tune your ears to wisdom, and concentrate on understanding. Search for them as you would for lost money or hidden treasure. Do not let them out of your sight; let them penetrate deep within your heart.*
> *Lay hold of my words with all your heart;*
> *keep my commands and you will live."*
> —Proverbs 2:1; 4:20; 4:4 NLT, NIV

I Think I'll Get Radical

I've spent most of my Christian life concerned about being *balanced,* keeping a degree of symmetry when reaching out to share Christ; lest I seem too *radical* in my faith. Of course, balance is always good; but after so many years of being concerned about balance, I believe I'd like to spend the rest of my life being just a little "radical."

These days in the more vociferous segments of our political/cultural society, "radical" is repeatedly being used to label folks—"far left radicals; far right radicals;" etc. Even one of our top legislators recently referred (disdainfully) to "those far right *conservative* radicals." (Meaning Christians like you and me).

We tend to equate being radical with being extreme; but that is only part of the definition. It actually can mean to <u>"go to the root of a thing</u>, to <u>the origin, the beginning</u>." A *true* radical Webster says, is *rooted*—well I like to think I'm rooted and grounded in the love of Christ! (Ephesians 3:17)

Actually, you could say Jesus was a radical...

He commanded us to love God with ALL our heart, soul, mind and strength—that's radical.

He commanded us to love our neighbor as ourselves—that sounds radical.

He said we are to preach the gospel (not necessarily Baptist, Methodist, Pentecostal or Catholic, etc. but the pure, unadulterated New Testament Gospel), to every person on earth and turn all nations into His followers...Now—some will call that *radical.*

I believe a "radical for Jesus" is one who defies the whims, even spiritual whims, (fallacies) of his day. If the Word does not validate it, or if that Word is taken out of context—exaggerated or minimized—I would surely call it a whimsical fallacy. A radical for Jesus, calls people back to *root realities* and *root causes* and resolutions, based on New Testament teaching…being *Radically Rooted* in The Word!

A radical may even become a *revolutionary*: progressive, radical, innovative, according to Webster.

**Revolutions happen when someone takes
radically, something that has always been there.
(Could this be a definition of revival)?**

The great revolutions in the history of Christianity did not occur by someone discovering something new…

—Martin Luther took the simple gospel message of justification by faith…radically.

—John Wesley took the simple message of biblical holiness…radically.

—William Seymour took the simple biblical promise of a present tense encounter with the Holy Spirit…radically.

—Billy Graham took radically, the simple Words of Christ, "You must be born again—go into all the world and preach the Gospel."

We need radicals *now, today,* who are anchored in Christ and His Word; with a desire to propagate the gospel with renewed courage and confidence. Nothing More…Nothing Less!

Will we be true radical followers of Jesus…*extremely* in love with Him, *extremely* devoted to Him, His Word and His cause?

The need is urgent, the time is short. Do you agree?…This is the day for us to take Christ's Great Commission and His commandments radically— let's do our part to start a revolution and pave the way for His soon return.

Let's get Radical for Christ!

Final Moving Day

"I'll have a new body; I'll have a new home." Those lyrics to a fun southern gospel song sound even better than usual to me these days; as I struggle with the aches and pains of moving, and getting settled! After 55 years of owning our home, we have reached a stage in life, numerically and physically, when it sounds easier and simpler to let someone else have the added responsibilities of maintenance and upkeep—not to mention taxes! Hopefully this will be our last move until heaven—oh glorious hope!

For now, as we apply our own personal finishing touches and settle in, this house will become *home* just as the one before this, and the one before that…I learned early on that a house is just a house—a man-made *structure;* it is the people dwelling within that make it a home—living, loving…*abiding.*

In reality, as we dwell on this earth, we are all just "renting." This world is NOT our home; our citizenship is in heaven. (Philippians 3:20; Ephesians 2:19) And *moving day is rapidly approaching!*

As our particular moving day approached, I thought I would be all packed and ready in plenty of time—I even knew the exact day and time the trucks would arrive—still it seemed to come SO SUDDENLY!* Our faithful caring helpers arrived, and we were moving—right now, ready or not! Fortunately, I had the opportunity to go back and forth to the old house for a short time, to finish up and do a final last minute check.

It's a lot like going to heaven—are you packed and ready? Better double check; when Jesus comes to "move us on up", there won't be any chance to "go back for one last check." We'll be traveling light—our spotless blood-washed robes of righteousness in Christ, are all we'll need. And just think,there will be none of the aches and pains of moving afterward! The moving arrangements are simple. He won't need your address; if you're sure Jesus is your permanent dwelling place. *"Lord, you have been our dwelling place throughout all generations…He who dwells in the shelter of the Most High will rest in the shadow of the Almighty."* (Psalm 90:1; 91:1) Are you truly *dwelling,* (abiding) *in* Him? *"In Him we live and move and have our being."* (Acts 17:28)

Perhaps God will call me "home" before the rapture—or perhaps you and I will be "caught up" to meet Him in the air. (1 Thessalonians 4:17)…I'm convinced that day will be very soon. All the things the Bible says must be in place before Christ comes for His church, ARE IN PLACE…Consider some of the more obvious—Iran developing nuclear bombs, Israel facing infinitely persistent threats, North Korea testing long-range missiles, Russia returning to their hostile attitude, China beginning to look like the world's bank and our own United States becoming more and more secular, not only politically—but in the prevailing world-view…even the church is becoming more and more secular.

If you read the Bible and watch the news—you are well aware that the time is near…We don't need any additional evidence that life on this planet is hanging in the balance. Jesus said, "When you see these things—look up, your redemption is at hand." (Luke 21:28) So, don't get too settled in and comfy here, we won't be here forever. And—we won't be taking any of our "stuff" with us! It won't be long now. However, Jesus also taught us that we are to occupy (do business) until He comes. "So be prepared (watch), for you do not know what day the Lord is coming." (Matthew 24:42 NLT)

Now friend…don't try to set specific dates for Jesus' return, or pay any attention to those who do…Don't put your confidence in the "signs," but have a watchful regard for them…And…Just Believe!

Jesus IS coming back! So—Live Like it!

Act Like it!

Watch—Pray—Occupy!

Studying and understanding the events of tomorrow, as outlined in scripture, will help you live with confidence and hope today.[37]

---

37 David Jeremiah, Turning Point Magazine, April 2013

Epilogue

As we finish this part of our journey through the *Seasons of Life*…Let's pause with praise on our lips, and His Word in our heart…

Praise be to the name of God forever and ever,
wisdom and power are His.
He changes the times and the seasons,
He sets up kings and deposes them.
He gives wisdom to the wise
and knowledge to the discerning.
He reveals deep and hidden things;
and He knows what lies in darkness,
And light dwells with Him.
I thank and praise you, O God of my fathers…
—Daniel 2: 20-23

~~~~~~~

Hope Lives On

A True Story

~~~~~~~

"If you lose hope, somehow you lose
the vitality that keeps life moving, you
lose the courage to be, that quality
that helps you go on in spite of it all.
And so today I still have a dream."

Martin Luther King Jr.

~~~~~~~

Preface

Hope is a condition of the heart and soul, a continual spanning of the seasons of life...Giving us the ability to live life to the fullest degree that our situation will allow, and even beyond.

Come along with me as I reminisce of another journey. At times a sad and difficult journey...made possible by clinging to the rock, God, the rock of our salvation, *"When my heart is overwhelmed; lead me to the rock that is higher than I"* (Psalm 61:2) This is not my journey, but Berniece's...A story of love and hope. I walked alongside and watched in awe as God guided her each day—with *her* hand in His.

I learned so much as I walked this road with Berniece...about God's sovereignty and the importance of leaning on His arms of grace, standing fast on the Word—sometimes in desperation, but always in faith and sincere hope. I invite you to come along on her journey. As I reminisce, I pray you will be encouraged by the many accounts of His faithfulness. Each step of the way, God has provided the necessary strength, wisdom, support—and HOPE...through His Word and prayer. In the beginning, none of us had any idea where the road ahead would take her, but we were sure God had a pathway in mind. *"Righteousness will go before Him, and shall make His footsteps our pathway."* (Psalm 85:13)

Berniece is my younger sister, this is her story...a story of dreams crumbled, joy removed, hopes challenged. Yet it is also a story of *new dreams* realized, *joy restored,* and *hope renewed,* all by the gentle hand of our God. Each day as you and I pray, "Your Kingdom come, Your will be done," we are saying, "God, I desire to have Your priorities established in my life today."...We pray expectantly with hope, faith and trust in an Almighty God and His sovereign will. Believing that He knows the end from the beginning always gives us confidence that

He will guide us along the best path to fulfill His will in our lives… even when the road seems impassable.

I pray as you read her story you will be able to see the Lord's fingerprints on the pages of Berniece's life. Whatever circumstances you are facing right now, I ask the Holy Spirit to encourage you to believe HOPE LIVES ON!

Hope Lives On

Blessed is he whose help is the God of Jacob,
whose hope is in the Lord his God.
—Psalm 146:5

It was a bitter cold evening in our little northern town. Inside our home however, pleasant warmth filled my heart. As I prepared dinner for our family, I had a cozy feeling of gratitude as usual. It was an ordinary evening; Dad was in his chair in the living room with his newspaper. Our seven year old daughter, Billie Jo was in the kitchen "helping Mom" with dinner by setting the table. Ten month old Tina sat *not so patiently* in her high chair waiting to be fed—vociferously letting me know she was getting a little unhappy about the wait…she was a little too young to understand the value of all us sitting around the dinner table together—as a family…we were truly blessed!

When the phone rang, I quizzically wondered *once more* why God hadn't made mothers with three hands! The somewhat less-than-tactful voice on the other end of the line shouted (or so it seemed), "It's your sister; she's been in a head-on auto crash! Yes, it is, *very* serious, they don't expect her to live—yes, yes, she was alone, her husband and baby were at home; they've taken her to the local hospital."

More than forty-nine years have passed since Berniece began her unexpected journey; a journey that has intertwined our lives for many years. In the meantime, our children have grown, married and presented us with grandchildren. Like most families, ours has experienced both the good and not so good—marriages and divorces; heartaches and happiness; sadness and joy; tragedy and triumph. Our parents, eldest brother and youngest sister are gone now. But through it all—there's remained the perpetual belief that God's Will never takes us where His grace can't keep us. No one held more persistently to that belief than Berniece. The events following that fateful January day in 1964 will always be with us like a beacon of hope—hope eternal.

As I hung up the phone, my cries brought my husband Bill to my side. "Oh, God, please don't let her die!"

Leaving our two girls with Bill's folks, we began the anxious eight mile trip to her side. Speeding was not wise; although the road was not as treacherous as it had been in recent days, it was still icy in patches. A heavy snowfall followed by sub-zero temperatures had caused it to be very dangerous; typical of Northern Wisconsin in January. Back then our highway was not the best of roads even in good weather. *I was keenly aware that we were travelling the very road which caused the accident that made this trip necessary.* Bill drove carefully and quietly, leaving me to my jumbled thoughts.

As I hoped, I prayed—and I remembered...I thought of Berniece's husband Dave and their ten month old daughter Kendra, their first child. Our Tina was just three days older than Kendra. Just ten months earlier Berniece and I had shared a room in the maternity ward of the same hospital where she was now facing death. *(Back then giving birth meant a five day hospital stay.)*

Even though nine years separates Berniece and me in age, we were very close. Most of our family lived in Rhinelander, Wisconsin, where we grew up. Both our husbands grew up in Tomahawk, about 20 miles southwest, and that's where the four of us resided, about four miles apart on Highway 86, just west of the city. Life seemed good.

Now my sporadic thoughts were going way back, remembering what a beautiful child Berniece had been—an answer to a nine year old girl's prayers. Being the oldest of three at the time, with two younger brothers, I was desperate to have a baby sister. Grandma had often said we can ask God for anything and if He knows it is good for us, we will get it. (In those days, nine year old girls were not too "up" on the specifics of how and when the gender of a pregnancy took place!) So I

170

prayed, and I believed—and in May 1943 my Mom presented *me* with a beautiful, angelic baby sister! Chubby but petite, with big, bright-blue eyes... I've heard it said that nearly *all* newborns have blue eyes in the beginning and many soon change color, but Berniece's just seemed to get bigger and bluer...When she was two or three, I would dress her all up and take her for walks to show her off—this toddling little beauty in a blue dress to highlight those sparkling blue eyes. How proud I was! As each additional sibling came along, I loved them all; but there always seemed to be a special bond between Berniece and me...Later, she would share many things with me—her first crush, her first kiss, her worries, her joys—the sort of things that seemed so *major, so traumatic* if you were a young teenage girl. It was so much easier to share with a big sister than with Mom.

Berniece came to love the Lord very young, but as all too often happens, in her teens she began to question some things about her Christian life-style. It was during this *questioning* stage, while visiting us in Tomahawk; she met David—and soon fell in love. They were married in less than a year; she was eighteen, he twenty-one. What a beautiful bride she was—As the wheels of the car clicked off the miles, I was remembering how Dave's face fairly beamed with love and pride as she walked toward him...Could that really have been less than three years before?

Dave had no knowledge of what it really meant to be a Christian, or have a personal relationship with Christ—he was baptized as a baby and identified with a certain "religion" by name, but followed non-committedly. After Kendra was born, I sensed Berniece was feeling a pull back to the Christian roots as she knew them. They began to attend his church and had Kendra baptized. Church going didn't last long for Dave, soon it was back to the same old routine...

Amid this patchwork of thoughts and tears, we had finally reached the hospital. There we found a distraught Dave, "She's unconscious and they don't really know why—they suspect brain injury!" Soon they told us the head x-rays didn't reveal any reason for her unconsciousness. Her physical injuries appeared to be minimal, inconsequential even—a

171

simple fracture to the collarbone and a laceration on the top of her hand. It had been necessary to perform a tracheotomy, which no doubt saved her life.

The unconscious state continued for days. Soon they were referring to her as being *comatose;* somehow that sounded more ominous than *unconscious*. Still, as friends and family kept prayer vigils, hope reigned in our hearts. Our sister Molly, two years younger than Berniece and out of school, came to care for baby Kendra and to keep their home going. What a blessing she would be to all of us. Over the coming months she would frequently and ably, take care of my family as well, so I could be available when necessary to follow Berniece's progress.

By the fifth day, the doctors and staff of our small hospital hadn't been able to find an answer; they didn't seem to know what to do except wait for her to regain consciousness. We could not accept that… Arrangements were made to transport her to the hospital in Wausau, Wisconsin, about 60 miles south, where a neurologist and more testing procedures were available. It was determined something was causing pressure on her brain, perhaps fluid, perhaps blood. Surgery would be required to relieve the pressure "as it could be causing brain damage," they said.

Surgery revealed the pressure to be fluid buildup, which was not as threatening as blood—that might have caused clots, stroke, even death. Unfortunately, the prognosis was not good. They removed the fluid through two holes surgically bored through the skull. When they had done all they knew to do, she still remained comatose. Doctors were still unsure how much brain damage might have been sustained or how permanent it might be. Forty-nine years ago, even the hospital in Wausau was not the modern, well-equipped facility it is today.

I was determined to stand in the gap for Berniece, with prayer and the Word of God. I truly believed that was where we would find hope; as Paul says in Romans 15:4: *"For everything that was written in the past was written to teach us, so that through endurance and encouragement of the scripture, we might have hope."* As her proxy, I prayed daily as I thought she would pray: *"Sustain me according to your promise and I will live; do not let my hopes be dashed."* (Psalm 119:116)

Her eyes were open, but fixed and staring; her body was without any voluntary movement, and there was absolutely no sign of any awareness of anything or anybody. She was now referred to as "semi-comatose". The decision was made to transfer her to St. Joseph's Hospital in Marshfield, Wisconsin, for examination by a neurosurgeon. After a few days of exhaustive probing, prodding, and perusing—the neurosurgeon summoned all immediate family available.

He began, "There may be more brain damage than first suspected; and there is nothing we can do to reverse it." I listened closely as he explained, "In all probability, she will remain in this vegetative condition indefinitely until one infection or another takes her life—it could be weeks, months, or possibly even years. We will keep her here for a few weeks and continue to observe her. In the meantime, you will probably want to look into nursing home facilities...." With that, the doctor's voice seemed to trail off, as if it came from the far end of a tunnel—barely cutting through the cloud of despair attempting to settle over me as I tried to listen..."However," he continued, "I must remind you, I am only the doctor...I perform what my skills enable me to do and the rest is up to God." Suddenly his words were reverberating clearly...Glorious hope-filled words, resounding deep in my spirit—from a doctor...confirming that there is hope in God! The threat of despair had lifted, and once again I felt God's tendrils of grace wrap gently, but tenaciously around my heart with love and hope.

Now, I was concerned about Dave. I knew he was becoming more and more discouraged, and if discouragement doesn't give way to hope in Christ, it will foster bitterness. Bitterness will eat away at us until it destroys from within and will certainly rob our peace. I hugged my brother-in-law (who wasn't the "huggy" type) and said, "Try not to worry, Dave, we'll just keep hoping and praying." He nodded in agreement, but I knew he didn't really understand. I could see the frustration and the weariness take hold of him, but he continued to hold on. Berniece would be in Marshfield Hospital for about two months.

Dave worked five days a week and always made the 200 mile round trip on weekends to sit with Berniece. Most of those weekends little Kendra spent the day with our family while her Daddy was gone; she was much too young to understand what even we couldn't. This gave Molly the weekend off to go home to Rhinelander and "do her thing." During the week, Dave and Bill would have to tune-up his aging VW Bug to be sure it would make the next trip. Someone else in the family, as well as myself, always made it to Marshfield one or two weekdays. It didn't matter if she didn't know we were there....

One Sunday, my husband and I drove with Dave to see Berniece—I will never forget that landmark afternoon. All along the doctors had said she probably could not see, hear or understand us; nevertheless we chatted with one another as usual—as if she were a part of the conversation. Suddenly, we noticed her eyes were moving—focusing on us—this was a first! We sensed she might be aware of us—even hearing us! Perhaps even comprehending? I asked her to blink her eyes if she could hear me—she did! Oh, the childlike exuberance that followed! Directions for her to use one blink for "Yes" and two blinks for "No" began quite an intense cross examination! When she slipped into unconsciousness again, we panicked and called a nurse! As we related our astounding discovery, she took Berniece's vitals. She smiled and said, "I think you simply exhausted her—however, her new neurologist is going to be pleasantly surprised! He is having a difficult time giving up on this one." Much later we would learn from her that she had been aware of much of what was happening around her for some time, but was unable to respond.

I went back a few days later and happened to be there when the neurologist, recently assigned to her case, detected a very slight reflex in her feet. His words were like music: "I don't think this young woman should be sent to a nursing home quite yet. I believe she deserves at least a chance at rehabilitation of some sort." His suggestion was the University of Wisconsin Rehabilitation Hospital in Madison.

Arrangements were made, but there was a waiting list. Okay, *"Be still before the Lord and wait patiently for Him."* (Psalm 37:7) Since it would be at least a month, she was transported back to Tomahawk Sacred Heart Hospital to wait for the call. There, friends and family could visit more frequently, and perhaps she could see Kendra…and Kendra could somehow begin to know and accept her Mommy. However, it turned out the visits had to be short and limited as Berniece sobbed deep internal sobs the whole time, which frightened one year old Kendra. Regardless, without the long trips to Marshfield, it was easier all around to have Berniece closer.

It had finally been established unequivocally that she had brain damage to the motor center, the speech center *(they explained it as—the part of the brain that stores vocabulary, or the knowledge of words was functioning, but not the part that allows her to "speak" them).* Also there had been damage to the vocal chords. Although she was cognizant, she could not move any part of her body, and could not speak. The trachea tube still remained, which meant she could not swallow to eat or drink. BUT her mental abilities seemed to be intact, and she was in no unusual pain…How we praised our God for that blessing!

After six weeks in the Tomahawk hospital—on Memorial Day week-end, she was on her way to Madison. Because of escalating medical expenses, Dave, Bill and I headed for the Capitol City carrying Berniece in the back of a borrowed station wagon, comfortably tucked in on a borrowed gurney. We were told by the staff to get her settled in, say our goodbyes and head back home, "for her own good." She looked so small and helpless; she was never much more than five feet tall and a little over one hundred pounds; now after four months of only intravenous feeding, she looked pitifully frail—leaving her was very difficult. We knew she was frightened—in a strange place, surrounded by unfamiliar faces, and unable to say or do anything…Still, they asked that we not visit for two weeks.

Two weeks later when we arrived, we were stunned! She was sitting upright, strapped in a wheelchair. Special supports held her head up and fixed in one place; her arms were attached to a cross bar at the top of the chair with long, heavy rubber band-like straps so her arms flailed about involuntarily, and her feet were solidly fastened in place—she literally looked like a frenzied, life-sized marionette! At first I wanted to cry—and yet it was such a welcome and unexpected sight…from flat down in bed with no movement whatever, to this, in just two weeks!

She was in the chair only a few hours a day in short increments of time. Despite the progress, she was suffering a lot of pain; we were told that was a part of the process. Again, God spoke comfort through the Psalmist: *"My comfort in my suffering is this: Your promise gives me life."* (Psalm 119:50)

Once again Dave was making the long drive to see her, 200 miles one-way now. My husband and I often joined him. One additional positive was the opportunity to see some of the sights of our State Capitol, so on one trip we even took our (now) eight year old daughter.

In a few months' Berniece was making weekend visits home. She was now able to spend all her waking hours in her wheelchair without the arm or head supports. The tracheotomy tube was finally removed and now her throat could begin to heal. She had partial use of two fingers and the thumb on her left hand, enabling her to communicate by spelling out words with one finger on an alphabet board (writing would come later—and ultimately a computer). Her visits home became times of trial and error, all bequeathing joy and laughter as we learned together—and adjusted to *her* new lifestyle. She was taking *real food* now, "fed" through a tube surgically inserted through the abdomen into her stomach. Her food was freshly prepared each day in a blender, reducing it to a well-balanced liquid diet. It was "fed" into the tube with a *kitchen baster!* Berniece's sense of humor kept us all encouraged; she would gleefully try to "smack" her lips—mmm-mmm as she was being "fed."

In the beginning, Dave, Molly and I were the only ones who learned how to handle her. As you might guess (except for tall, strong Dave,) at one time or another in those initial days, Molly and I each accidently missed the chair, depositing her on the floor, and often ourselves down there with her! I managed that trick once when I had her halfway between the bathroom *"commode"* and her chair. Such blunders always resulted in her laughing at us from deep down inside—not much more than a *gurgle* for sound—but it was euphoric!. Once safely back in her chair, in an effort to ease our clumsy conscience she would spell out, "I won't break you know!"

Many memories were created in those visits home. Also, of course, many tears were shed, but many prayers answered as well. Tears— *spontaneous tears* had become Berniece's only means of communicating emotions—happiness, sadness, pain, disappointment, anger, and most of all—LOVE! I soon concluded that the longer she cried when she saw you, the more she loved and missed you. She did get that somewhat under control after a while. She also became very adroit at *speaking* with her eyes, those big beautiful blue eyes; they expressed much if one learned how to "read" them.

After about six months, all supports were removed except the foot braces; she was able to balance herself quite well in the chair, and she began to take a diet of soft foods. Soon she was released to come home permanently—they could do no more—she had reached a plateau…She was a quadriplegic who could not speak. She was only 21 years old; her husband Dave only 24 years old; their daughter 19 months. But praise God, she was alive and she was not a "vegetable" as first predicted! Her mental faculties were totally intact! *The only thing she could not remember was the accident itself, and to this day, she still can't—a merciful blessing.* She managed very well to say whatever she wished, even if she did have to spell each word by pointing out one letter at a time! *One day at a time,* she would choose to live out Romans 12:12…

"Be joyful in hope, patient in affliction, faithful in prayer."

"Hope is both the earliest and the most indispensable virtue in the state of being alive. If life is to be sustained hope must remain, even where confidence is wounded, trust impaired." —Erik H. Erikson

Yes, God had become Berniece's all in all—her shield and buckler, her strong tower, her shelter in the time of storm, and she could say, *"Though He slay me, yet will I hope in Him...(Job 13:15).*

After Berniece had been home about a year, Sister Molly got married, leaving Dave with very little help. He fell between the cracks for Community aid—not enough income to hire full-time care and a little too much to qualify for community assistance. His only help were those able to come while he worked, mostly volunteers. Working and caring for Berniece and a toddler day after day, Dave found it more and more difficult to cope. The constant 24/7 demands of caring for her, Kendra and their home; plus working a full time job was a heavy burden for any one person. Dave was young and virile, a good man, but a man who didn't know the Lord nor His strength *(Jesus said, "My grace is sufficient for you, for my strength is made perfect in (your) weakness." 2 Corinthians 12:9)* Dave did not know this—he was a man trying to get by on his own meager resources. So, when he reached the end of *his* resources, there was nothing more to draw from. Consequently, his physical, mental and moral endurance wore thin; the marriage finally ended by mutual consent with an uncontested divorce.

There is absolutely no doubt that Dave had loved Berniece deeply. I saw that love blossom. However, they were both still so very young. Human *(romantic)* love alone is seldom enough in the face of such challenges; it must be reinforced with God's *agape* love—"less an affection, more a decision; less a feeling, more an action"...(Max Lucado in LIVE LOVED—Thomas Nelson Publishing). A more specific definition of that is found in the "love chapter," 1 Corinthians 13, *"Love never gives up, never loses faith, is always hopeful, and endures through every circumstance (verse 7).Such love is available to anyone who chooses a personal relationship with Christ.* As Jerry Bridges says in <u>The Practice of Godliness</u>; "biblical love is not emotions or feelings, but attitudes and actions that seek the best interest of the other person."

In other words—<u>we *can love with God's love because His love can dwell in us...*</u>"*And hope does not disappoint us, because God has poured out His love into our hearts by the Holy Spirit.”* (Romans 5:5) In <u>A Love Worth</u> <u>Giving,</u> author Max Lucado reveals a very pithy secret as to how to BE loved, *“The secret to being loved is to <u>live loved</u>. This is the forgotten first step in relationships.”* (Ponder that for a while!)

Assured our family would take over their care, Dave agreed to let Berniece retain custody of their daughter, now nearly three years old. Our parents wanted to care for both Berniece and Kendra, and it seemed a good interim choice. However, within a year, Mother's health began to deteriorate; they all realized other plans must be made for Berniece...so Berniece made the choice to go to a nursing home. The timing was right for several reasons—there she would soon get a promising new kind of therapy developed at the Sister Kenney Institute in Minneapolis, Minnesota, where she had recently spent some time. The therapy required five persons to coordinate the procedure—how thankful we were for the wonderful volunteers at the Friendly Village Nursing Home in Rhinelander Wisconsin. However, the therapy did not prove successful, but at least she had made the effort.

As long as Kendra and her mom were able to be cared for in the same place, it was best; but now my husband and I would take over the care of Kendra with Berniece and Dave's full consent. She would be raised with her cousins, a good experience for all our family...Berniece always remained an integral part of Kendra's growing up years.

It would require a full-length book to relate those early years in detail. Although she put her trust for the future in the hands of her Savior, Berniece never became complacent, or gave up. She endeavored to follow any avenue that might be God's pathway to her miracle—the various hospitals, new therapies—each offering hope upon hope; unfortunately in Berniece's case, none were the answer. In her first year home she, Dave and I travelled to Chicago's beautiful McCormick Place for an Oral Roberts Crusade. Several years later, as guests of a beautiful couple in our church, she and I made another trip to McCormick Place for a Kathryn Kuhlman Crusade...but that road to recovery was not a part of God's plan either—the experience was spiritually awe-inspiring, but not the miracle He had in mind for her.

Berniece was in a nursing home for about 15 years. During that time she acquired so many new and caring friends, some residents in the home, many outside... I'd like to once again say thank you and God bless you...to the many people who helped sustain her in the years that followed; I wish I could mention them all by name At times we still think of her fellow residents also, both young and old, who were often inspired by her enduring peace, joy, faith and hope.

Several residents, near the same age as Berniece, were *paraplegic* and *very bitterly* struggled with the *why* of it...Though she persistently encouraged them, they never chose to reconcile to their situation or to God, and *take* His peace. All three passed away a number of years ago. We hope and pray they found their peace with God beforehand.

Berniece's faith in God and her hope for the future never wavered. Instead of asking, "Why God?" concerning what she had *lost*...at each turn she yielded to His *Sovereignty.* That isn't always easy for any of us; perhaps because we can't seem to *accept* the full meaning of the word in reference to God. Author Jerry Bridges puts it this way, *"This is the essence of God's sovereignty; His absolute independence to do as He pleases and His absolute control over of all His creatures".*[38] That seems difficult to reconcile with the picture of a totally loving God...Yet just such complete acceptance of His sovereignty is what brings His peace; followed by a joy that is not found outside the realm of God's grace. Only as we accept God's love, and return that love can we know what peace lies in accepting His sovereignty. Berniece is so grateful to Him for *what she still has* as well as for *what she has gained.*

Shortly after Kendra came to live in Tomahawk with our family, Berniece moved from the Home in Rhinelander to the Golden Age Nursing Home in Tomahawk. Every Sunday we went by "The Home" to get Berniece for church...during the summer, our girls walked the

---

38   Trusting God, by Jerry Bridges (NavPress, 1988)

few blocks with her as she "drove" her electric chair from The Home to the church. (With the partial use of two fingers and the thumb on her left hand). However, the chair did not fold and as the weather grew colder, we had to use the folding chair and transport her in the car. Soon Berniece would enter a new phase in her unusual life...

As Kendra and Tina grew into adolescence, Berniece acquired a new friend...Ron was a man near her age who attended our church. He was a good Christian man, who was raising his young daughter alone with help from her grandparents. Because ours was a small church, my family had known him for years. One winter Ron began offering his help in getting Berniece in and out of our car at church. It was a challenging feat for me, but he lifted her from the car to her chair and back again in one swift swoop! As their friendship steadily became closer, they discovered a number of things they had in common, including their love and devotion to Christ.

> *Ron worked on the Soo Line Railroad, and was only home in the late fall and winter months. Those were the very months we had to use the folding chair, loading it in and out of the trunk, as well as getting Berniece in and out—so his help became a real blessing.*

Ron was becoming Berniece's Knight in Shining Armor—I began to notice she literally glowed when he was present. It seemed to give him joy to help her in any way he could. I saw that Ron had a deep desire to be *wanted* and *needed*...We were seeing an act of God in progress! As their friendship continued to grow, Ron began spending a lot of time visiting at The Home. You've heard the cliché "the miracle of love." Well, this truly was a miracle...the miracle of God's love bestowed. Just two souls needing something, finding it in each other and coming together—each for different purposes, with different needs, but the same love—God's love!

Around this time, because of Bill's work my family and I moved to Rhinelander, so Berniece considered moving back to the Home in Rhinelander. However, she chose to stay in Tomahawk, she had been there for years, and didn't want to change—I was very sure Ron was also a factor in her decision.

In 1981, Kendra and Tina graduated from Rhinelander High School. Exactly one week later, our older daughter Billie Jo married. One *year* later, Kendra married—AND—the *following year,* Ron and Berniece were married. She had now been handicapped for about nineteen years- -in a nursing home for about fifteen years. Ron was 46, Berniece forty years of age; young enough for many good years together. They became a family in a home of their own, along with his daughter Roxanne. Their relationship gives affirmation and credence to the phrase *the bond of love*—a bond man cannot explain, this joining together of two hearts...one man, one woman—neither of them *quite whole* in themselves, coming together in marriage, to become "whole" in Jesus Christ. That's a fact no mathematician or scientist can explain!

I thank God every day for Ron—a beautiful brother-in-law and a true brother in Christ. Of course it is not a one way blessing. Berniece has brought to Ron's life many things he had needed for years...some that are often taken for granted...needs that can only be provided by a devoted heart and soul. It has been a blessing to see the joy they share as they face all of life's challenges together.

> Perhaps some of you have been waiting for the chapter in this story that finally proclaims the miracle of healing—the part where Berniece gets up and walks or begins to talk! You will not find that particular miracle—but I pray you do see the amazing miracle that has taken place because of one brave, young woman who chose to love and trust God no matter what...a miracle happened not only for her, but for many around her.

The years have passed happily for Ron and Berniece. He retired in 1999. His daughter has been grown and on her own for years. Ron and Berniece continue to enjoy a happy life together. They still share their love for the Lord, and most of their aspirations are toward Him and others. God has provided all Ron will need to go on caring for Berniece and himself well into old age, *which has craftily crept up on all of us.* They are a joy to watch—Ron has become her voice; he can quickly read her eyes as well as every gesture (I believe he can often even read her mind). When all that occasionally fails, she resorts to spelling words!

Over the years, Berniece has gained so much more than she lost in that one tragic moment. More in fact, than many of us who are physically whole. Christ brought to her life a kind of fullness no one, even she could have imagined.

In the beginning, it was sometimes difficult *not* to ask, "Why Lord?" *If only she could just speak...if only......*But hope doesn't dwell on the negative, hope trusts in God's sovereign will, even when we don't understand. Hope doesn't dwell on the problem, hope accepts the solution God has chosen, realizing *He* does indeed *know the end from the beginning*—and He does *not* make mistakes. Both Berniece and Ron are very familiar with God's *"peace that transcends all understanding."* (*Philippians 4:7*) And as He promised in Isaiah 26:3, "He *has* kept them in perfect peace...because they trust in Him." They not only trust Him in all things, but they have *loved Him with all their heart, soul and strength.* (Deuteronomy 6:5)

Frances Roberts sums it up quite well in <u>Make Hast My Beloved</u> (written as God speaking):

> "A loving heart is a vessel of light and mercy. It is a receptacle into which I pour My grace. It is untarnished by avarice and indifferent to the call of worldly ambition...There is no safety in external circumstances. The only shield for the spirit of man is My presence...My presence is experienced not by how you *feel*, but how you *believe*. It is your *trust* that brings you near to Me. I am always with you, as I promised I would be. Your *awareness* of My presence is in proportion to your confidence in me. If you find it difficult to trust, then LOVE Me. Love bridges every gap and leaps over every mountain. It is the ultimate cure for every ill."[39]

---

39   Make Haste My Beloved, by Frances J. Roberts—Barbour Publishing.

Berniece and Ron can attest to that!

This woman, whose prognosis was to be a living vegetable until she died a young death; has seen her daughter grow up and give her two grandchildren and joined her heart and spirit with a loving, lifetime partner. She has enjoyed good general health and wellbeing (considerably better than all her siblings)! And as she ages, Berniece is quick to tell you, life is good—so very good!

This story opened with a quote from a speech by Martin Luther King Jr. "If you lose hope, somehow you lose the vitality that keeps life moving, you lose the courage to be, that quality that helps you go on in spite of it all. And so today I still have a dream." This quote sums up Berniece's life—attitude...her philosophy...

She enjoys telling others *the reason for the hope that she has. (See 1Peter 3:15)*... That hope will live on...and one day she shall see her Lord face to face. And I truly believe, in that glorious moment when she *WALKS* with Him, and *TALKS* with Him—which of course she will...she won't be asking "why", but like the healed paralytic in Acts *3:8-9,* she will be "walking and jumping and praising God!" With her new voice she will SPEAK the name of Jesus over and over. She will sing, she will shout—glory and honor and praises, to her King of Kings and Lord of Lords—who has been her everlasting strength and her eternal hope...**a Hope that lives on!**

"We have this hope as an anchor for the soul...
the hope that is laid up for us in heaven."
Hebrews 6:19; Colossians 1:5

Aim for heaven and you'll get earth thrown in,
Aim for earth and you'll get neither.
—C.S. Lewis

A simple bumper sticker states it so profoundly:
KNOW GOD—KNOW HOPE
NO GOD—NO HOPE

An update...

Ron and Berniece owned a home in rural Brantwood, Wisconsin, about thirty-five miles from Rhinelander. From the time of their marriage in 1983 until he retired in 1999, Ron followed his work for the Railroad. Berniece travelled with him nearly every spring and summer—by choice. They tried live-in care at home, but she preferred life on the road *with Ron!* Wherever the road took them, God graciously provided a place to stay, and whatever help was needed for Berniece while he worked. Just one more way God proved His lovingkindness, as He provided her with multiplied grace and endurance.

By the time he retired, both their daughters were settled into their individual lives in other parts of the country, and after a few years they had no family in the Brantwood area. So, six years after retirement, they decided to sell their home and move to Rhinelander. They now reside very near me, a blessing of convenience for each of us.

When Ron retired, Berniece hosted a lovely retirement party with the help of church friends. I want to leave you with a loving picture of this "treasure" of a man...a tribute I wrote at the time of his retirement on behalf of all Berniece's family....

February 14, 1999

To Ron—In Loving Tribute...

He travelled from the near obscurity of a backwoods farm in Brantwood, Wisconsin—to most of the big cities and the small towns across America's Midwest—wherever the rails stretched, crisscrossed or ended, he would go. For thirty-five years he labored faithfully and diligently to help keep the wheels of the Soo Line Railroad turning on safe tracks. This boy of proud Finnish heritage had become a man—a husband—a father—and a railroad man. He wore each title with pride, dedication and success.

Our family's path crossed Ron's nearly thirty years ago—that's a long time, long enough to know what a really special person is this man called Ron Keto...father, husband, friend and brother...a man after God's own heart.

As a family, over the years we have been blessed of God with numerous and diversified blessings...none more special, miraculous *nor more timely* than the bringing of Ron into Berniece's life. The expression "God-send" can sometimes be used a little loosely—but it is the only truly descriptive and appropriate word for the bringing together of these two.

God always knows the "whys" of life, even if He doesn't reveal them to us...*"I know the plans I have for you says the Lord, plans for good, not for evil, plans to give you a hope and a future."* (Jeremiah 29:11) If they trust Him completely and follow Him obediently, the Rons and Bernieces will always be brought together by the hand of God.

They had sixteen springs and summers together on the railroad—often difficult and tiring for both, but always with the peace of mind and contentment that they were together—and God was with them.

We all honor Ron today; but we, Berniece's family, want to honor him with our special love and gratitude—for loving Berniece with enduring, unconditional love that comes from the heart of God...For taking her into his life, and of course, for allowing all of us to tag along—no brother can be more treasured.

Ron, we wish you many years of good health, peace and content-ment. Only God can reward you for the years you've given of yourself—to so many, most of all, Berniece. God presented the challenge, you accepted, met and exceeded the challenge—*He* will reward you.

Ron—we love you, appreciate you, and Praise God for you!

Berniece's Family

Afterword...

It can be a good thing to be the "eldest," or the "matriarch" as one brother sometimes called me...the love and respect of my family is one of the dearest treasures I have on earth.

This past year Ron and Berniece (as well as others) have become God's hand extended toward *me* in many ways as I've faced life without my help-mate. We three just 'keep on keeping on;' following whatever path He puts before us. We will always have *"the hope that does not disappoint us, for God has poured out His love into our hearts by the Holy Spirit whom He has given us."* This is our source of strength, peace, joy and contentment—every hour..."*while we wait for that blessed hope—the glorious appearing of our great God and Savior, Jesus Christ."* —Romans 5:5; Titus 2:13

Until then—my heart will go on singing!

About the Author

For years, Virginia (known mostly as "Ginna" by friends and family), has been writing a featured column, "The Barnabus Factor" and "A Moment with Ginna," in _Grace Lines,_ a newsletter for the church she attends. Her prose and poetry have been shared in various formats but never before professionally published. Her determination to walk life's pathway with her hand firmly in God's, has given her the desire to seek a deeper, more intimate relationship with Christ; which she hopes every child of God will desire and experience. Recently widowed, she lives in Rhinelander, Wisconsin. Her grown children, grandson and other family live nearby.